LIFE IN
STUART ENGLAND

Staghunting

Life in
STUART ENGLAND

MAURICE ASHLEY

English Life Series
Edited by PETER QUENNELL

LONDON: B. T. BATSFORD LTD
NEW YORK: G. P. PUTNAM'S SONS

First published 1964
Second Impression, 1965
Third Impression, 1967

© Maurice Ashley, 1964

Made and printed in Great Britain
by William Clowes and Sons, Limited, London and Beccles
for the publishers
B. T. BATSFORD LTD
4 Fitzhardinge Street, Portman Square, London, W.1
G. P. PUTNAM'S SONS
200 Madison Avenue, New York 16, N.Y.

Contents

Author's Note

For the benefit of readers of this book I would like to express my personal opinion that the value of money in the middle of the seventeenth century was fifteen to twenty times what it is today. But I must add that most historians of the Stuart age would not be willing to commit themselves to any multiple whatsoever.

I am deeply obliged to Professor Austin Woolrych of Lancaster University for reading the book in manuscript and saving me from a number of errors. In revising the text for the third impression I have taken particular account of the recent books by Peter Laslett, Lawrence Stone and Charles Wilson (listed on pages 20 and 80).

Acknowledgment

The illustrations on pages 92 and 98 are reproduced by gracious permission of Her Majesty The Queen.

The Author and Publishers wish to thank the following for the illustrations appearing in this book: the Ashmolean Museum, Oxford for pages 4, 14, 62, 115, and 163; the Trustees of the British Museum for the frontispiece and pages 57, 67 (top), 70, 86, 89–91, 102, 110, 123, 125, 130, 138, 153, 154, and 171; the Church Missionary Society for page 59; the Guildhall Library, Corporation of London for page 150; A. F. Kersting, F.R.P.S. for page 122; the London Museum for page 161; the Mansell Collection for pages 46, 132, 136, 144, and 170; the National Maritime Museum, Greenwich for page 58; the National Portrait Gallery for page 148; the Corporation of Oxford for page 119; the Royal Academy for Arts for pages 72, 98, 119, and 161; the Sussex Archaeological Society (Ann of Cleves House, Lewes) for page 9; Sir Anthony Doughty Tichborne, Bt. for page 72; the Trustees of the Victoria and Albert Museum (Crown Copyright Reserved) for page 41.

The Illustrations

England in the Seventeenth Century

~ARTHUR BANKS~

Map showing places mentioned in the text

A Panorama of England

Life in Stuart England, during the century or more that stretched from the enthronement of King James I in 1603 to the death of Queen Anne in 1714, is lit up by striking contrasts and by a slow progress in the accumulation of national wealth, in the arts of parliamentary government, and in the acceptance of new lines of thought. The greatest contrast of all was between the heights of individual wealth—the nobility enjoying incomes averaging in the mid-century £5,000 or £6,000 a year, obtained from rents, offices, and investments, or merchants and professional men with carefully acquired capital ready to be handed on to their children or to charities—and the depths of poverty, men and women with barely enough to live on, earning wages of a shilling or less a day, and hundreds of thousands dependent on the poor rate or on charity. Another contrast was between ancient superstitious beliefs, as in alchemy, witchcraft or the value of out-of-date classical lore, and the growth of a new scientific spirit, ranging from the teaching of Francis Bacon and Dr William Harvey to the discoveries of Robert Boyle and Sir Isaac Newton. Conservatism still held sway over the mass of men, as it always does; it was most notable in the practice of medicine and in methods of farming; and at the outset of the seventeenth century England possessed all the characteristics of an under-developed country.

Yet potentially it was (as it long had been) an opulent land with much fertile soil, with varied mineral resources, with the riches of the oceans everywhere near at hand, and a mild climate, except for occasional horrible frosts in mid-winter.

An age of relaxation

But broadly—again as has generally been the case except in times of crisis when there has been a challenge to which they could respond — the majority of the English people were lazy from top to bottom. King James I spent most of his time hunting or pontificating; his grandson, King Charles II could only be induced to pay attention to business in short bursts. Even the single-minded King William III was said to have grown 'remiss and careless' in his last years, while it was complained that Queen Anne was too devoted to playing cards and drinking tea. The gentry followed the example of the Court; many of them passing their daylight hours in hunting, drinking, and over-eating; as the years passed by, the arduous duties of a justice of the peace tended to be concentrated in the hands of an assiduous few. A civil servant like Samuel Pepys managed to school himself to stop leaving his office to go to a theatre or a coffee house in the afternoons, but he was an exceptional character. A shopkeeper would put up his shutters and receive complaints about his absence from the villagers; agricultural labourers, though supposedly toiling from dawn to dusk, would play games in the shade or the alehouse if they could; and if they were invited to mend the roads or local bridges to facilitate transport, they preferred to loiter around and do nothing. During the first half of the seventeenth century many of the clergy did not preach. Soldiers and sailors stopped fighting from October to May. Parliaments did not meet every year and sessions lasted only two or three months. The country gentlemen who formed the bulk of the membership of the House of Commons had no desire to be detained at Westminster during the spring or at harvest time. Officials hung about waiting on the monarch, while their duties were incompetently performed by deputies. So life rolled lazily on.

Its customary course was frequently interrupted by early if not unexpected deaths. London was regularly decimated by plagues. Few families escaped smallpox. Women often died in childbirth and the odds must have been about even that any given child would survive the first year or so of life. In towns lack of sanitation contributed to disease, while physicians and surgeons were pretty expert in killing their patients. Tuberculosis or rickets was the common lot of the poor. But there is little evidence of starvation, as in France. The average expectation of life at birth was not high and the country was full of widows and widowers marrying and remarrying. The affluent built their magnificent houses and planted their stately trees over their broad acres not for themselves but for their posterity; the poor quaffed their pints of ale when they could afford them and looked for a much happier existence when they were dead. A few men, like King Charles II, believed in being as merry as they could while life lasted and trusted that God would not condemn them for a few small sins; but most Englishmen—not merely the Puritans—were obsessed by a sense of sin after they had enjoyed themselves and believed with Sir Walter Raleigh that they would be punished for doing so in this life as well as in the next.

One must not exaggerate the static character of English life under the Stuarts. Adventurous men and minds emerged from time to time. If one would hesitate to assert that the rulers of England were moved by the noble considerations for the welfare of its citizens that inspired a Pericles or Cicero, one must remember that two significant political revolutions took place during the century, in 1642 and 1688, killing all chance of despotism; and, as we shall see, there were many examples of

Townspeople fleeing into the country from the plague of 1630

scientific enlightenment, economic advancement, and colonial experiment. One historian has claimed that an industrial revolution culminated in the reign of King James I, others that the reign of King Charles II witnessed the death of medieval thought. There was no lack of fresh ideas in religion or in political theories, in art, in music, and in physics. Culture reached a high level among the educated classes, especially poetry. But change was not rapid in the ordinary structure of life. Queen Elizabeth I might have found herself a little uncomfortable at the Court of Queen Anne; but one doubts if a peasant or an agricultural labourer who never moved out of his native village—unless swept up into the wars—would have noticed much difference. As Peter Laslett has written, 'the truth is that changes in English society between the reign of Elizabeth and the reign of Anne were not revolutionary.'

AN ECONOMIC MAP

No exact statistics exist for the seventeenth century, although the birth of modern statistics is usually assigned to the reign of King Charles II, when Sir William Petty and Captain John Graunt, the first 'political arithmeticians', flourished, and they were followed by Gregory King, whose estimates of population have been the subject of controversy ever since. But most seventeenth-century statistics, even those of wages and prices, contain a conventional element. It may be hazarded that the population of England and Wales at the outset of the Stuart period was between four and four-and-a-half million: of this about 300,000 were concentrated in London, that is to say, more precisely, the City of London, Westminster and certain outlying suburbs. The next largest towns, Norwich and Bristol, each contained fewer than a tenth of the population of London. Both Norwich and

Sir William Petty (1623-87)

4

Bristol were ports as well as centres of cloth manufacture and market towns. Most county towns comprised from 400 to 600 households. London was not the focus of English life to the extent that the statistics suggest or as it is in modern times. It is true that the government of the country functioned for most of the Stuart period from Whitehall and that Parliament met at Westminster. But the Court moved about the country, while parliaments met irregularly. The City of London had only four members of parliament, though there were two for Westminster and two for Southwark. Both the English counties and most of the English boroughs were represented at Westminster by leading country gentlemen who came up periodically almost as the ambassadors from foreign countries to speak for their peoples. The counties were often referred to as 'countries' and dinners were regularly held by county representatives gathered in London to remind them of home. 'The provinces of England', Dr W. G. Hoskins has written, 'were incomparably more individual and distinctive than they are today. The landed gentry still spoke, not the standardized speech of a social class, but with all the rich variety of their native parts.' Not only had they their own language, but the counties had their own aristocracy, administrations, and cultures. Roads were extremely bad: in many places it took days for orders and instructions to arrive from London. The lords lieutenant of the counties and the members of parliament visited the capital from time to time, but they did not necessarily have houses in London; indeed some of the great men in the counties preferred to have a second residence in the county town.

Not only was there a notable contrast between London and the provinces, but also between the northern and southern parts of England. For centuries wars had been fought across the Scottish border and much of the north of England was primitive and unruly. The accession of King James VI of Scots as King James I of England gradually reduced this historic tension. For the first time the wealthier inhabitants of the north of England began to build themselves ordinary manor houses instead of castles or 'peel towers' designed to protect them

5

against marauders. But it was not until 1707 that legislative union between England and Scotland was completed. In the reign of King Charles I (1625–49) the monarch found it easier to recruit soldiers in the north in an effort to impose his wishes on his Scottish subjects because they were so accustomed to fighting the Scots; during the civil wars Scottish armies thrice invaded the north of England, reviving angry memories of the past. So these counties were inured to lawlessness. Roger North described how in the reign of King Charles II when his relative, Lord Chief Justice Francis North travelled from Newcastle upon Tyne over a 'hideous' road to Cumberland he had to be provided with arms and guards.

The north was, on the whole, poorer, less populous, and less civilized than the south of England. In the counties bordering on Scotland cattle thieving was a commonplace until the Act of Union and highwaymen were regularly at work on the coach roads, being supplied with information about well-to-do travellers by confederates in the inns. In Westmorland feuds between the families of the Musgraves and the Lowthers still persisted. York, with a population of eight to ten thousand, was a civilized town that long held out for the King during the civil wars and by the end of the century Newcastle was one of the most prosperous towns outside London; not only a port, but a centre of the coal, salt, and glass industries. In Northumberland one of the first railways in English history was to be found. Five chaldrons of coal could be drawn by horses along wooden rails from the colliery to the river Tyne.

The cornlands of East Anglia:

Though important pockets of industry and manufacture existed throughout the country, as at Newcastle, England was still essentially agricultural. Even London had a rural setting: Piccadilly was still countrified when the century began. Throughout the Stuart era many families divided their time between weaving or spinning and tillage. It has been estimated that four-fifths of the population was engaged in agriculture including sheep-farming while, Dr Wedgwood suggests, a great many of the King's subjects derived their living wholly or in part from the sea. It is also

The Exchange at Newcastle, built 1655–8

reckoned that about half of the country was under cultivation or pasture; the rest consisted of moorlands, swamps, or forests. Some of the forests were preserved for the benefit of royalty and other huntsmen and in the reign of King Charles I forest laws were still a popular grievance. Very slowly waste or common land was brought under cultivation or enclosed by arrangement largely for the benefit of the bigger farmers. Riots against enclosures both of the waste- and of the fen-lands were frequent in the first half of the seventeenth

Harvest time

century. Roughly the eastern half of England was cornland (wheat, barley or rye), while much of the west was pasturage. But there were fine pastures in East Anglia, and Devonshire contained some of the richest fields in England. Mixed farming, in the technical sense of the term, did not exist, but 'even in regions where tillage predominated practically every farmer owned some sheep' (Mildred Campbell).

Thus, to return to the north of England, we see in Cumberland and Westmorland the bulk of the inhabitants drawing their livelihood from fishing or keeping sheep. But in Kendal there was an active woollen cloth industry. Cumberland was typical border country where the people were described by Roger North as 'comical', but in Carlisle good ale and beer were brewed; at Kendal in Westmorland, again according to Roger North, 'a scattered town very stony and dirty . . . the common people walked barefoot and the children leaping as if they had hoofs, and these shod with iron; but it is almost the same all over the north'. In Northumberland too fishermen and shepherds predominated, but in Yorkshire Leeds, famous for its breweries, and Sheffield, already a centre of cutlery manufacture, were promising industrial towns, and the manufacture of cloth was important in the West Riding. Durham and Northumberland contained iron industry and there were salt pans in Cheshire. Yorkshire was said to be richer than Lancashire; but in Manchester the cotton industry had its beginnings; here fustians (a mixture of wool and cotton) were made for workmen's clothing at the outset of the Stuart period. Lancashire was a centre of Roman Catholicism long after the

Silversmiths at work

old religion had been proscribed. Liverpool, a small port, formed a link with Ireland, and during the civil wars the Royalists tried to bring over Irish soldiers by this route. Hence Roman Catholicism persisted there until the present day. The Royalists commanded many supporters both in Lancashire and Yorkshire, and established families remained loyal to the Stuarts even after the Hanoverians came to the throne of England.

A Sussex ironfounder

The north of England during the Stuart period probably contained about a quarter of the population and wealth of the nation. The more sophisticated and cultured people of the south were reluctant to visit or settle in the north, as they still are today. Monarchs only stopped there on their way to Scotland or if driven there, as was King Charles I. London and the counties immediately surrounding it were the most populated parts of the kingdom and also the wealthiest; apart from Yorkshire, which was the largest county, Middlesex, Somerset, and Devonshire were, according to the tax returns, the richest counties.

In the south of England Kent was one of the most highly cultivated counties. At harvest-time labourers had to be imported from outside to help, and they were well paid; Kent was famous for its hops, fruit, and grain; but the seasonal scarcity of labour was due to the fact that many men who lived there were employed at sea in fishing, commerce, or the royal navy. Chatham and Gravesend offered naval employment; much traffic and many travellers reached London by sea, and Gravesend was the gateway to the capital. Sussex was then famous for its iron ore, and during the civil war its forges were kept busy. Farther west Somerset and Devon were prosperous counties, for not only was their soil fertile, but they were busy cloth-making districts. In the Mendip Hills of Somerset lead and coal mines were then active: the miners were violent, lawless,

Bristol, the second city in the country: 'a large city,

and hard-drinking men. Cornwall still had an important tin industry; it provided 'irregular and often sweated employment to ten to twelve thousand miners, who lived in huts and worked in short shifts (often by candlelight)' (Ogg).

These southern counties were full of seamen and fishermen. Some of them sailed in the latter half of the century regularly to Newfoundland for the valuable cod-fishing. At Plymouth it was reported by a traveller in the reign of King Charles II that only women and children were to be seen since the greater part of the men were living at sea. At Exeter, capital of Devon, a town with a fair-sized population, besides the manufacture of baize and other light cloth, there was a cottage lace-making industry. In Devon and Dorset the cattle were celebrated and 'of prodigious quantity'. Wiltshire was renowned for its dairy farms as well as its cloth industry. (Often the two went together.) Many active little ports were scattered along the south and south-west coasts, some of them doing legitimate business, others profiting from smuggling, notably in exported raw wool and imported wines and brandies. But the only port to offer any comparison with London was Bristol, described by a seaman in the middle of the seventeenth century as 'a large

great trade, the streets very narrow'

city, of great trade, the streets very narrow, so it seems never intended for a great place when it was first built'. It was able to sell direct the goods which its merchants brought home and to export cloth overseas. 'Its carriers supplied all South Wales, the south-west, and the western midlands with sugar, wine, oil and tobacco' (Bryant).

Wales was a relatively backward country in the Stuart period, keenly Royalist in the first half of the century, but becoming much more puritanical as the years wore on: a great effort was made by Major-General Thomas Harrison, the fanatical 'Fifth Monarchist' leader of Cromwell's time, to convert the Welsh people to his way of thinking. Over half a century later when Daniel Defoe visited Wales, he found the country as a whole 'dry, barren, and mountainous' though he took note of the cattle of Cardiganshire and the shipping at Milford Haven. He observed that 'provisions were very good and cheap, and very good accommodation in the inns' and 'that the Welsh gentlemen are very civil, hospitable, and kind'. Gloucestershire, like Somerset, had its share of industry, for in addition to textiles, coal and iron mines were being worked.

The west Midlands concentrated largely on sheep farming,

11

both for wool and for meat, but Bedfordshire, Hertfordshire, and Berkshire had wheat and barley fields as well as cattle. Leicestershire was rich in corn and contained fine sheep and bad roads. East Anglia was an increasingly prosperous part of England, the home of many rising gentry, who studied the markets and knew when to buy and sell. Much knitting and spinning went on in the cottages of Norfolk and Suffolk, which were famous for their worsteds. Peterborough in Lincolnshire was described by the adventurous lady traveller, Celia Fiennes, at the end of the seventeenth century as being a fine clean city, 'a very industrious, thriving town' with 'spinning and knitting amongst the ordinary people'. Norwich, the chief town in Norfolk, was reckoned the second largest city in England after London. Ipswich in Suffolk, on the other hand, had no manufacturing and therefore ships that unloaded there had to be sent empty away. In the fen country, which covered much of East Anglia, tremendous efforts at draining were made especially in the reign of King Charles II (1660–85), although the work, sponsored by enterprising capitalists, was resisted by 'an indigenous race of fen dwellers, the Slodgers, who in spite of chronic agues contrived in their huts of wattle to maintain a semi-aquatic existence by snaring, fishing, and reed cutting' (Ogg). Though considerable progress in reclaiming the watery wastes had been achieved by 1670, Celia Fiennes, when she visited the area 30 years later, noted that the inhabitants were 'a lazy sort of people and afraid to do too much'.

Broadly the eastern corner of England was fortunate in that it had a more mixed economy than most parts: it manufactured a variety of woollen textiles; it did well out of fishing (in those days oysters and lobsters were cheap and plentiful), and it also engaged in ship building. After Norwich, Colchester was one of the busiest towns in eastern England, for besides being a fishing port, it was able to send its cloth for sale to London, only 42 miles away. Colchester boasted 16 churches and Norwich had 36.

A fen-labourer using a trenching spade

But most of East Anglia was strongly puritanical and retained a tradition of dissent after the restoration of King Charles II. French Protestants had settled there from the beginning of the century and immigration increased when King Louis XIV involuntarily drove them out in the 1680s. Protestant Dutchmen came there also and settled in these flat, watery lands, so like their native country. Their skill and industry contributed materially to enriching these parts of England.

DEPRESSIONS AND BOOMS

When King James I came to the throne a 'price revolution' was still in full swing. This had been caused partly by the influx into Europe of precious metals from the New World. The general price level is believed to have risen about fourfold since the beginning of the sixteenth century. In England food prices continued to rise pretty rapidly until about 1620. This had various consequences: first, since prices rose more quickly than wages, which were to some extent artificially kept down by law, real wages tended to fall, hitting the poorest classes. At the other end of the social scale it reduced the value of the Crown's customary revenues, which inclined to be inelastic. Big landlords, on the other hand, were less affected; it is true that their rents could not always be easily increased because of the existence of long leases, but there appears to have been swift rise in landed incomes after the 1590s during which rents began catching up with prices. Sheep farming was still extremely profitable at the outset of the Stuart period: in East Anglia and Northamptonshire, in particular, landowners enjoyed a substantial increase in their agricultural incomes and found pasture a very profitable investment. It has been estimated that between 1600 and 1640 the rents of pastureland increased threefold and arable land in East Anglia sixfold. Sometimes the sales of sheep as stock yielded more than wool. It was not surprising therefore that there was a vigorous demand for land. It was only during the Interregnum (1649–60), when Crown and Church lands had been sold in large parcels, that its price began to fall.

13

Sheep farming in East Anglia

From the 1620s onward the demand for wool for the manufacture of cloth declined. A prohibition on the export of undyed and undressed cloth in the interests of a monopoly conferred by the King had a damaging effect on the cloth export trade; foreign competition was growing fast; and the civil wars further interfered with the cloth industry. During the reign of King Charles II it was complained that wool was being overproduced and was declining in quality. Increased competition arose with Holland in the manufacture of finished cloth and with Spain in the output of high quality wool. Nevertheless the main English export was cloth throughout the Stuart period and, if such statistics as exist may be trusted, the value of cloth exports had risen substantially by the end of the seventeenth century. Other exports included metals, such as tin and lead, salted fish and other foodstuffs, when the harvests were good, and smuggled raw wool. But towards the end of the Stuart period the most valuable exports after cloth were goods obtained from outside Europe, for example, spices from the Far East, imported by the East India Company, or tobacco and sugar from the colonies established in the West Indies and North America, which were re-exported to Europe at a profit.

But on the whole England was self-sufficient. Many households grew their own food, produced their own drink, and made their own clothes. Luxuries were imported for the benefit of the rich, while exports consisted largely of food, raw materials, and semi-manufactured goods: a typical pattern in underdeveloped countries. During the century violent economic

14

fluctuations persisted. These were determined not merely by changes in the world price level, but by the weather as it affected the quantity of the harvests, by wars that interrupted trade, and by the incidence of plagues, particularly in London, through which most of the foreign trade of the country flowed. In the first year of the reigns of both King James I and his son the capital was severely hit by plagues that killed over 30,000 persons on each occasion. During the period 1606–10 the London theatres had to be closed on account of plagues. In 1634 there was a smallpox epidemic and in 1638 both plague and smallpox. In the year before the outbreak of the civil war the capital suffered many deaths from typhus as well as smallpox and plague, while plague persisted throughout the 1640s. The last 'Great Plague' was in 1665 when nearly 70,000 Londoners died of it.

Economic setbacks occurred in the early 1620s, in 1640, and in 1659. Again, in the 1670s there was a phase of bad harvests, economic depression, and bankruptcies. Wars do not seem to have stimulated trade; usually an economic recovery took place when peace temporarily supervened, as in the first half of King James I's reign, during the early part of the Cromwellian Protectorate, after the Anglo-Dutch wars in Charles II's time, and as the War of the Spanish Succession neared its end in 1710.

In view of all these interruptions and uncertainties it was not surprising if economic expansion was slow. In the first half of the seventeenth century agricultural production tended to stagnate, exports were sluggish, the cloth industry fluctuated, even

London during the Great Plague of 1665

catches of fish were not high, except for herrings that proved hard to dispose of. As real wages fell or at any rate stayed low in the first half of the century, the demand for industrial products was largely confined to a few. The well-to-do tended to stick to land as the safest form of investment; but liquid capital must have been scarce, for it was not until 1651 that the rate of interest was reduced to six per cent. As Professor F. J. Fisher has written, the main features of the English economy up to 1640 were rising food prices, low wages, and growing pauperism.

In the second half of the century the national economy received a stimulus from an increase in commerce, in shipping, and in other services. Already, before this time, English ships were being more largely used for carrying purposes, except in the Baltic trade. On the eve of the civil wars it was established that the activity of British shipping had expanded tenfold over a period of 30 years. Excise and customs revenues expanded during the Protectorate and again after the depression of the late 1660s. The price of wool rose after 1678. Re-exports were in demand abroad, while gradually the wealthier classes were induced by the lower interest rates and the golden promise of commerce with colonies and trading posts abroad to invest

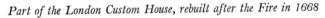

Part of the London Custom House, rebuilt after the Fire in 1668

their money otherwise than in land. Merchants and the rising professional classes had funds to spare for speculation. The coal and iron industries proved worth investing in as well as merchant adventures. Modern banking and insurance methods were gradually evolved and the Bank of England successfully established in the 1690s. People began to keep their money in banks instead of under their beds. At last the commercial and industrial monopolies beloved of Queen Elizabeth I and King James I were being broken and trade restrictions loosened. There was a general relaxation in the laws governing apprenticeship. In spite of the continued backwardness of English agriculture, which after the restoration of King Charles II had to be protected by restrictions on the import and bounties on the export of corn, the progress of capital investment and the advances in exports and in services had by the reign of Queen Anne given a real impulse to the nation's economy. This was reflected in an increase in population. In the eighteenth century the availability of capital for investment, the improvement in international trade, and long periods of peace paved the way for a technological revolution, as well as an agrarian one.

Yet all this had developed slowly. One is inclined to think of the reign of King Charles II, the Merry Monarch, as an idyllic age in English history. 'The quiet years of Charles II's reign,' wrote his admirer, Sir Arthur Bryant, 'between the Civil Wars that had passed and the great wars that were to come, were marked by steady mercantile and colonial expansion. Men were laying up for themselves and their children treasure for the future. On every sea the adventurous ships of England sailed, returning with riches in their holds to enhance the wealth of the little island of squires, yeomen, and homely merchants, and bringing silks and delicate cloths for their ladies.' 'The post-Restoration atmosphere', observes Mr Christopher Hill less lyrically, 'was conducive to capital investment and scientific experiment.' But agriculture, which remained the way of life for the mass of the English people, did not yet show much advance. It is true that the Royal Society and a number of authors offered suggestions for improvements. The use of clovers on pastureland was suggested; variations in the rotation

17

of crops were advocated; fertilizers of one kind and another were considered; a traveller from Flanders drew attention to the value of the turnip as a cleansing crop and a winter food for cattle. But in actual fact the only fertilizer in common use was lime; the usual rotation remained the traditional two crops followed by fallow; the common use of the turnip, except as a vegetable, had to await the eighteenth century, at any rate outside East Anglia; the potato was still neglected. Landlords, protected by the new corn laws and rejoicing in the absence of land taxes, remained conservative. According to Pepys, 'our gentry are grown ignorant in everything of good husbandry'.

While an essential harmony prevailed between a satisfied landowning squirearchy and the rising industrial and commercial magnates—never before was there so much inter-marriage between the children of merchants and gentry—the real wages of labourers and husbandmen remained stagnant or even fell. Gregory King estimated that the yearly income per family of 'cottagers and paupers', numbering 400,000 in 1688, was £6 10s. a head. The poor rate then cost the nation between £900,000 and £1,000,000 a year. All the evidence suggests that there was a considerable amount of general and casual unemployment which enabled wages to be kept down. Poverty was particularly marked both in the towns and villages. It has been reckoned, for example, that there was an unemployment rate of 16·8 per cent in Lichfield at the end of the seventeenth century. 'By the second half of the seventeenth century,' writes Dr W. G. Hoskins in his study of a Midland village, 'it is clear that we have "the poor" as a permanent feature of the village community. They were emerging as a class and a considerable class at that. . . .' The enforcement of the laws against the able-bodied poor became harsher than ever and there was probably less private charity than before the civil wars. Both the old forest laws and the new

Beggars

game law passed in 1671 placed difficulties in the way of the poorer people
obtaining meat, though no doubt poaching continued. For all these reasons
much underlying social discontent
existed, which sometimes came to the
surface in rioting. In 1670 a band of
marauders, calling themselves Levellers, appeared in Worcestershire;
indictments for riot and trespass were
common at quarter sessions. A few
instances of strikes and machine-
breaking are on record; criminals were
numerous and robberies frequent.

Daniel Defoe (1661–1731), a brilliant industrial reporter

It is not in fact until the very end of
the Stuart period that one receives the
impression of improving social conditions or public disturbances that were motivated by religious and political excite-
ment rather than economic dissatisfaction. The colonial and
commercial gains that England won because of the Duke of
Marlborough's victories in the War of the Spanish Succession
(1702–13) and the triumphs of the British navy on the oceans
resulted in a wider diffusion of wealth. 'The age of Anne', it
has been said, 'was the prelude to a long era of content.' A
greater division of labour was then taking place; more retail
shops came into existence; more employment became available
through the increase of industry and shipping; during the long
wars labour actually became scarce; and with the opening up
of commerce with parts of the former Spanish Empire and with
the establishment of the union between England and Scotland
trade circulated more freely. The picture of the country painted
by that brilliant industrial reporter, Daniel Defoe, indicated a
widening prosperity in which most classes participated. More
white bread was then being eaten; more ale and cider were
drunk; industry was more active; an excellent postal service
had been established; credit was more easily obtained through
the banking system; on the whole, the harvests were good and
an agrarian revolution was not far off.

Thus, in spite of fluctuations and periods of abysmal poverty and distress, the Stuart period was one of general social and economic progress. People generally were materially better off in the reign of Queen Anne than they had been in that of Queen Elizabeth I. The rise in population, which reached five and a half million in England and Wales, including perhaps half a million in the capital, reflected improvements in the art of medicine and sanitation and also less malnutrition and actual starvation among the poorest subjects of Queen Anne. A more diversified economic structure offered opportunities to all sorts of Englishmen. Social discontent receded. Ahead lay the comparatively peaceful era of Sir Robert Walpole.

Further Reading

Max Beloff, *Public Order and Popular Disturbances 1660–1714*, 1938
Andrew Browning (ed.), *English Historical Documents 1660–1714*, 1953
Arthur Bryant, *The England of Charles II*, 1934
G. N. Clark, *The Wealth of England 1496–1760*, 1946
Christopher Hill, *The Century of Revolution, 1603–1714*, 1961
Peter Laslett, *The World we have Lost*, 1965
Wallace Notestein, *English People on the Eve of Colonization 1603–1630*, 1954
G. M. Trevelyan, *Illustrated English Social History*, 1950
C. V. Wedgwood, *The King's Peace 1637–1641* (illustrated), 1955
Charles Wilson, *England's Apprenticeship 1603–1763*, 1965

II

Ordinary People

The ordinary people who made up most of the population of Stuart England—labouring people and out-servants, cottagers, paupers and vagabonds, common seamen and soldiers, according to the categories of the statistician, Gregory King—are too often forgotten. They lived on an extremely low level of income and a vast gulf divided them from the prospering gentry. On the whole, their standard of welfare seems actually to have declined after 1660. The paternalism of the early Stuart period was no longer practised by the post-Restoration governments. The total burden of the poor rate rose to an exceptionally high figure at the end of the seventeenth century. In Devonshire one-fifth of the population was on poor relief; in Cambridgeshire statutory wages rarely met the needs of a large family. John Bellers, a Quaker who is considered by some to have been one of the earliest English authors to propound socialist ideas, drew attention in 1699 to disturbances by silk weavers in London and to corn riots in other parts of the country. Though there was little articulate complaint outside London, where riots by apprentices were sporadic, evidence exists of an under-swell of social discontent. The amount of poor relief that had to be paid out, the grumbling that was heard from those who were obliged to pay it, and the restrictions imposed by parish authorities in an attempt to keep down the rate all suggest that poverty was increasing and widespread.

Sometimes in the reports of cases brought before quarter sessions a latent resentment rose to the surface. 'I care not for the constable or the King', observed a labourer in Yorkshire

A countryman

in 1616. 'The Devil go with the King and all the proud pack of them, what care I!' exclaimed a village blacksmith there in 1633. To an agricultural labourer it was natural enough to equate the village constable with King James I, for both were the voices of authority. But the constable was in fact one of themselves. He was often a tradesman or 'husbandman' who was chosen to undertake unpaid service for a year under the close supervision of the justices of the peace. The petty constable was indeed the linchpin of social life in rural England. 'The parish makes the constable,' wrote John Selden, 'and when the constable is made, he governs the parish.' By his fellow villagers he might at times be treated as a joke, but the higher authorities regarded him seriously enough and piled duties upon him. In theory he was supposed to be a substantial citizen; in practice the office rotated among the farmsteads and cottages of each village. Though the constable was not paid a salary, he had ample opportunity of taking fees and making a little money on the side. But it was a risky post, for the incumbent might be hit on the head by malefactors or pushed about by inebriates in the local alehouse. He was expected to watch out for vagabonds, to protect the private property of the well-to-do, to prevent trespassing and poaching, to see that order was kept in the taverns and inns, to catch petty thieves, to dispose of illegitimate children, to keep an eye on apprentices, and to ensure that both local and national taxes were punctually paid.

These were heavy obligations for an amateur. Sometimes village constables might be strong and competent men; in a poem entitled *The Song of the Constable* (1626) written by James Gyffen, himself a village constable in Surrey, he said:

> *A Constable must be honest and just,*
> *Have knowledge and good report*
> *And able to strain with body and brain*
> *Else he is not fitting for aught.*

But as often as not the constables who, as Gyffen also wrote, might go unwillingly to quarter sessions, regarded their duties as troublesome and difficult and had as their main objective to avoid reprimand or punishment from above.

Yet here in their work we perceive the real nature of the framework of English society 300 years ago. The aim of government was to protect private property and to prevent disorder and crime. The second was the condition of the first. In order to ensure stability, the poverty-stricken and the cripple

Inside a country alehouse

must be provided with the bare necessities of life out of the parish funds lest they turned to crime. Tramps and wandering thieves must be detected and thrust outside the parish boundaries. Those responsible for bringing illegitimate children into the world must be compelled to pay for them until such time as they could be apprenticed. And the better-off tradesmen must be obliged to accept such as apprentices. Alehouses had to be kept under surveillance lest they became nests of crime, gambling, or evil-doing. Convicted criminals had to be dispatched to the county gaol and hopeless invalids to hospitals or almshouses. During the periods of plague special watches were set up—

Husbandry

men being hired for the purpose—to prevent plague-stricken people from entering the parishes and to cordon off houses where the plague had penetrated. Thus was society kept safe from its own sicknesses.

The parish often contained more than one village. While the petty constable was a village official, responsible to the high constable and the justices for the adequate performance of his many duties, the clerk, the beadle, the sexton, and the well-master were parish officials under the direction of the churchwardens, who were usually gentry. This then was the typical little world of the ordinary man. The church and the alehouse were his social meeting places; the ducking stool, and the pillory, or the stocks were his danger signals; in the distance loomed the houses of correction and the county gaol.

In theory at least, ordinary men and women were at work all day long except on Sundays or the frequent public holidays. Even the skilled tradesman, the carpenter, the mason, or the blacksmith would have his own plot of land to till, a cow to milk, or hens to feed. His wife would have a brood of children to look after, the food to collect and prepare, the cottage to tidy and clean. On Sundays, outside service hours, games were permitted under the first two Stuarts, as defined in King James I's Book of Sports, but there were lawful games—such as archery—and unlawful games, like football. The average villager had a streak of sadism in him. Football, in which the entire village could take part, was an extremely rough sport in which bones could be broken. A crowd would gather to taunt the criminal in the stocks or to watch the public whipping of

Blacksmiths

some unfortunate woman who had given birth to an illegitimate child. Strangers were made unwelcome and treated with discourtesy. In London and the larger towns there were much frightening roughness and cruelty so that peaceful folk did not dare to venture out at nights into the ill-lit streets.

A vagabond

THE TREATMENT OF THE POOR

The treatment of the poor was usually extremely harsh. The Elizabethan poor laws, rendered necessary by the ending of the charitable care provided by the monasteries, were based on the principle that the helpless should be assisted, the unemployed set to work, and the incorrigible vagabonds severely punished. It would be wrong to say that genuine attempts were not exerted to fulfil all three parts of this programme during the Stuart period, but, on the whole, the main effort seems to have been directed to punishing vagabonds and kicking them out of the parish so that they should not become a local responsibility. Each parish had its overseers of the poor (generally men of yeomen class) who worked under the supervision of the churchwardens and the justices. With the approval of the justices a poor rate could be levied and money paid out to the helpless. After the bad harvests of 1629 and 1630 when there was much suffering poor rates were generally increased. In Somerset, for example, they were doubled or even trebled, and wealthier parishes were required to assist those which were overrun with paupers. The funds raised were also used to purchase stocks of raw materials to set the able-bodied poor to work. The Book of Orders, published by the government of King Charles I in 1630, was largely aimed at putting teeth into the administration of the poor laws; and undoubtedly for a time poor relief became more generous. Attempts were also made at this time—the period of 'personal rule' by King Charles I—to persecute hoarders of

Treatment of the poor: whipping a vagrant

foodstuffs and to exercise a tighter control over alehouses. Hunger riots had occurred; and once again one can see the intimate connection between the general economic situation and the concern of the ruling classes to preserve public order. The justices were then compelled to take action lest discontent got out of hand. The immediate effect of the Book of Orders was striking: 'the impotent poor were better relieved. The masterless poor were set on work. The apprentices were bound out, and if not always well treated, at least taken off the parish rates. Vagrants were, to a far greater extent than before, shown the error of their ways and recurrently locked up and removed from the concern of society' (Thomas Garden Barnes). During this period also there was a generous outflow of private charity towards the poor; in ten counties alone nearly a quarter of a million pounds was assigned to the establishment of almshouses.

Nevertheless few people in authority recognized in the Stuart period that poverty and unemployment might be involuntary; it was too often attributed to deliberate idleness or vice. Parish officials concentrated their attention on pushing the dependent poor outside their boundaries so as to pass on the responsibility to others. An Act of 1622 authorized the justices quickly to send back anyone who had not a decent cottage in which to live and whose family was likely to fall on the poor rates to the parish where he had last lived or worked. It was officially suggested that hordes of vagabonds were moving about the country looking for parishes where they might hope to receive the most generous treatment. If the parish officials were unable to eject poor people, then they were sent to 'houses of correction' or 'bridewells' which in theory were workhouses; in practice these became supplementary prisons. Under the Act of 1662 informers were rewarded for drawing the attention of churchwardens or constables to the presence of any rogues or sturdy beggars in their midst. Servants had even to produce testimonials from their masters to show to churchwardens and constables to prove that they were in gainful employment, otherwise they were liable to be whipped as vagrants and thrust out of the parishes. And thus the poor and the weak were frequently treated with unnecessary cruelty.

An agricultural labourer

WAGE EARNERS

Those who were in work mostly received meagre wages. Wage rates were laid down by the justices, and though in times of full employment they might not have been enforced, in many cases they certainly were. A typical daily wage rate for an agricultural labourer during the seventeenth century was 8*d.* or 10*d.* a day. The soldiers of Cromwell's army received the same rate. Skilled labourers like thatchers, masons, and carpenters might earn more, although in Yorkshire in 1658 their average wage seems to have been a shilling a day. Among women, apart from midwives, dairymaids were the best paid, but most women were lucky if they earned 4*d.* a day; thus it hardly paid wives to go out to work, although spinning was done by them in cottage homes. Wages were sometimes supplemented by 'godspennies', a small down payment when employment began.

A farmyard

These extremely low wages (low in money terms) should not be judged purely on their face value. For one thing most families worked as a unit. Comparatively modest families might boast servants and apprentices. Wives helped, when they could, in the fields, gardens, or shops. Children were set to work from a very early age. Secondly, nearly all cottages had a piece of land on which to grow food or feed cattle. Inventories that have survived show that small tradesmen and labourers usually owned hens, pigs, cows, and even bullocks. It was during the winter when it was difficult to keep animals alive that the threat of hunger or malnutrition was greatest.

In theory every cottage was supposed to have four acres of land attached to it, and attempts to enforce this law were made when new cottages were built. But it is extremely doubtful if this rule in fact prevailed. Certainly when parish authorities themselves put up a cheap wattle-and-plaster hut for some deserving family they did not provide them with four acres of

A northern village: Cleveland in Yorkshire

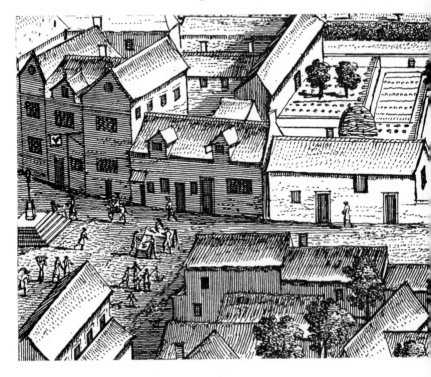

land. But where the four acres existed, there was no reason why a family should not be more or less self-supporting when the weather was good.

FAMILIES AND SEX

It has been estimated that the size of the average family was about four-and-a-half persons (excluding servants and apprentices who lived in). Although, in the absence of birth control, many children were born, only a few of them survived. Ordinary families could not afford to employ doctors or midwives; many babies were stillborn; others soon perished of childish diseases or of malnutrition. Ordinary men and women did not marry very young; first, they could not afford to do so; secondly, the parish authorities were watchful that marriages did not take place until couples were assured of a proper home to live in and so were not liable to come on to the poor rate. Until they married young women either worked for their fathers or were employed as domestic servants or nurses in wealthier households. Young men had to complete their terms of apprenticeship before they could command the prevailing wages. Probably as a rule men did not marry before they were twenty-six or women before they were about twenty-three. The gentry married rather earlier than that and the nobility sometimes at a very early age.

Since the age of marriage came relatively late it was not uncommon for the village lads to get the village maidens into trouble. Both in the records of the church courts and of the quarter sessions there is plenty of evidence that 'incontinence' before marriage and the birth of bastards in fair numbers was usual even in Puritan times. The authorities were extremely strict about illegitimate children not so much because of their sinfulness as because, if they were not careful, the parish—even the constable himself, if he could not pin the blame where it belonged—might have to pay for their upbringing. So both men and women regularly appeared before local courts charged with various sexual offences. As an instance, Helena Stanton of St Ebbe in Oxford was accused of 'scolding in service time and incontinence'. She claimed that William Dawson had promised her marriage and 'she yielded herself to him and fears she has child'. Even those who offered shelter to the unlucky women who gave birth to illegitimate children were liable to find themselves hauled up before magistrates' courts and fined. It was natural enough for women to be tempted and for men to go too far. But quite a few women were careful of their reputations and insisted on marriage. The circumstances of village life were such that everybody knew what everyone else was doing and it was easy enough for the constable to pick up the gossip in the alehouse.

When weddings took place it was a grand occasion for the poor. The neighbours rallied round to contribute what they could and the couple might experience a display of generosity from their employers or landlords. But afterwards for the average wife it was a life of toil and suffering. If she worked outside the home she was lucky to earn more than a few pence a week and it cost her as much as that to feed her husband if she had to buy food. It has been said that the agricultural labourer himself seldom went hungry, but 'the full misery of the labourer's lot was only felt by women'. If they were deserted by their husbands, they would be driven from parish to parish as nuisances and public burdens. But desertion seems to have been unusual; for women were really indispensable to a working-class family. Not only did they do all the feeding and clothing of the family, but they often supplemented the family income by spinning or seasonal work in the fields. Yet their incessant toil and regular output of unwanted children made them old long before their time. And for women who erred it was a cruel world. Here is a case from the Lancashire quarter sessions as recorded at the beginning of the seventeenth century:

A housewife working in the fields

William Dobson of Tarleton, husbandman, shall keep Alice, his bastard daughter until she is 12 years old. He and Anne Wildinge to be whipped this day at Ormskirk. Henry Dobson of Tarleton becomes surety for William. Anne Wildinge is to be flogged. Before she is released she must find surety for a moiety of the expense for keeping her child.

FOOD, DRINK AND CLOTHING

What did ordinary people eat and drink? A farm labourer who started work at dawn might have breakfast at half past six— usually bread and beer—dinner about midday, and supper at six in the evening. His meals would often be provided by his employer, but then his wages would be correspondingly reduced. One modern historian has claimed that 'compared with other countries, the English common people fed magnificently'. Daniel Defoe, in the reign of Queen Anne, declared that 'English labouring people eat and drink, especially the latter, three times as much in value as any sort of foreigners of the same dimensions in the world'. But that was at the end of the Stuart era. A good deal depended on the size of the family, on the quality of the harvest, and the time of the year. Gregory King thought that about half the population ate meat every day and most of the rest ate meat at least twice a week. But that certainly did not apply to the numerous unemployed.

The principal diet was bread, usually made from rye and not wheat. The average household could obtain eggs or bacon or, with luck, catch or snare wild fowl which was plentiful in forests and marshes. Not much cooking was done in the cottages, although a broth might be produced from beans or leftovers provided by landlords. Fish might be caught in the numerous streams and rivers. But penalties for poaching were severe. The early winter months were a bad time of the year. For meat and fish had to be eaten fresh, since the price of salt or spices for preserving food remained prohibitive. After Christmas starvation threatened. Then, one imagines, cheese was the chief stand-by: the inventories of husbandmen's goods mention large quantities of cheese stored in attics. But neither fruit nor

31

Sowing and fishing

vegetables seem to have been much eaten, even though they could be grown in cottage plots. And potatoes, later to become the staple food of the poor, were still unheard of or despised.

As to drink, ale was enormously consumed. Since very early times a large part of the tillage of the country had been devoted to barley for brewing. The usual price of best ale in the seventeenth century was a penny a quart, so that it was possible to get drunk for twopence. Cider was also popular in the western part of the country, while perry was a cheap drink. Tea and coffee were not known; cows did not yield a great deal of milk and it was mostly made into butter and cheese: in any case milk was enjoyed only by children and invalids. Spirits, such as gin, did not come within the reach of ordinary people until the eighteenth century. So ale was virtually a necessity of life. Variety was lent to it by spicing, warming, or sweetening. The local authorities recognized its importance by trying to fix and maintain a standard price for it. Thus beer, bread, and cheese were the staff of life, as they have long since remained. But since in the Stuart period vegetables were not very popular—boiled cabbage and the like being regarded, understandably, as 'windy meat'—the meals eaten by the average man would scarcely meet with the approval of a modern dietician.

We know a little about clothes from inventories. For instance, a widow left three gowns, five petticoat skirts, a 'safeguard' (an apron or overall) and cloak, two hats, three waistcoats, and 'wearing linen and other necessities'. In one case a woman's wardrobe was valued at nearly five times that of her husband's, who was a peasant. A typical man's outfit was a doublet, a hat, a pair of leather breeches, a pair of woollen breeches, a jerkin, two shirts, four bands, and two pairs of shoes—total value ten shillings.

The cottages in which labourers dwelt were 'in many cases flimsy huts built of clay and branches of trees and often without a chimney or any outlet for smoke except through the door'. Windows were rare, for glass was expensive. Most such houses contained only one or two rooms with a loft or attic. The main room was called the hall; the bedroom was described as a chamber; sometimes a chamber was divided into two as the size of a family increased. There might also be a kitchen and an outhouse or buttery. An upper floor was unusual, but lofts were used for sleeping in. An Act of 1589 had forbidden more than one family to live in each cottage; some evidence exists that cottagers could not or would not find room to house their ageing parents.

The main items of furniture were a long oaken dining table with stools or benches to sit on. Chairs were comparatively rare and not very comfortable, and were reserved for the head of the household or a guest. Chests rather than cupboards were used for storing clothes and household goods. Cheap collapsible 'trundle' beds with feather or flock mattresses were the usual thing; for by this time even the poor had ceased to sleep on straw pallets on the ground. Kitchens contained a wide variety of pots and pans; food was generally eaten off pewter plates with wooden spoons. The kettle or cauldron was an important cooking utensil; one inventory mentioned seven of them. Logs were the usual form of fuel for heating (if logs were unobtainable, cow dung or furze might be used)—though coal might be burned in areas within the reach of outcrops—and such lighting as there was came from rushlights or candles. The sanitary arrangements were primitive.

A labourer's cottage

SPORT AND PASTIMES

The mass of the people worked too long hours to find much time for recreation. At the beginning of the period

Morris-dancing

the royal government was still encouraging shooting at the butts and men were supposed to drill with the county militia, although that was rather a perfunctory business. Shooting fowl, rabbits, or foxes was a necessary occupation of the peasantry, but scarcely a sport. Dicing and card-playing became commoner as the years passed, but there is little evidence of the domestic manufacture of playing cards. Vaulting, dancing, and leaping were permissible on Sundays under the early Stuarts, but the traditional picture of the English peasant spending much of his time in country dancing is, one suspects, exaggerated, although Richard Baxter, the Presbyterian preacher wrote that in Shropshire in his father's time: 'In the village where I lived the Reader read the Common Prayer briefly, and the rest of the day was spent in dancing under the maypole and a great tree not far from my father's door where all the town did meet together. . . .'

Football was a village game, while stool-ball and cricket were coming in. Roger Lowe, a literate Lancashire apprentice whose diary for the early years of Charles II's reign has survived, played or watched bowls from time to time. Bowling alleys and greens were quite common and money was staked on the game. 'I went to a bowling alley', wrote Lowe in September, 1663, 'and lost 12*d.* at which I was sore grieved.' He also recorded how he watched a cock fight and hunted with hares. Cock-fighting and bear-baiting were popular sports in Stuart London,

Minstrels outside an alehouse

cudgel-play and wrestling in the country. During the period of Puritan supremacy a ban was imposed on many such games. Philip Stubbes had even disapproved of 'the horrible vice of pestiferous dancing'.

Village entertainment: a performance by strolling players

The alehouse, however, was essentially the poor man's club and meeting place. The justices of the peace kept as tight a hold over it as they could and it was closely watched by the village constables. Alehouses required a licence. The licensee was supposed to close his house early, to shut on Sundays, not to allow customers to stay drinking for longer than an hour, to prohibit dicing or gambling, to ensure that the ale was of good quality and a fixed price, and to keep out undesirables. Taverns, inns and, above all, fairs were visited by wandering minstrels and entertainers. Probably the licensed ale-house was as respectable as the modern public house; but unlicensed and solitary alehouses were haunts of criminals and vice.

RELIGION

What was the religion of ordinary people in Stuart times? This has never been the subject of detailed historical research. It has been rather easily assumed that they were ready converts to the Puritan *mores*. But *a priori* it would be more reasonable to suppose that they were conservative in their tastes and beliefs —their grandfathers had been accustomed to the Catholic ritual. They were expected to attend church services on Sundays, but no doubt looked forward to their leisure afterwards; it is hard to believe that they really enjoyed prolonged sermons. One doubts if the very poor went to church at all; but much may have depended on the vicar of the parish. At one parish in Nottinghamshire it is known that all the communicants turned up at Easter in the year 1676. The church was one of the twin centres of village life, and just as in St Paul's, London, on

Dancing round the maypole

Sundays and festival days 'the boys and maids and children of the adjoining parishes' would 'after dinner come into church and play as children used to do till dark night', so one imagines that parish churches were also not merely places of worship or set prayers, but shopping and gossiping centres. The Church Ales and other traditional festivities connected with parish life, such as dances round the Maypole, were bright spots in a drab existence, until halted by the Puritans. Writing in 1633, the Bishop of Bath and Wells noted that—'the chiefest cause of the dislike of these feasts among the preciser sort is because they are kept upon Sundays which they never call but Sabbath days, upon which they would have no manner of recreation, neither roast nor sod.'

Speaking of the period before 1640 Professor Wallace Notestein observed: 'As for the humbler classes, the Puritans had not yet awakened to the possibility of evangelizing them.' But they soon set about it. Nonetheless of the main Puritan groups the Independents and the Quakers initially made most impact on small gentry and tradesmen and those who might be described as lower middle classes, while it is hard to imagine that the Presbyterians with their firm belief in predestination (however modified) and their emphasis on a stern moral discipline appealed immediately to the mass of easy-going Englishmen. As Milton wrote, new presbyter proved to be old priest writ large. It has been claimed that in those days men 'bought sermons with the avidity with which they today buy detective stories' and that everyone read the English translations of the bible. But did they? In the Bedfordshire inventories there is only one mention of a bible, while one wonders how many villagers were in fact literate: certainly not half of them were, and probably fewer still.

However, it is true to say that as the civil wars loomed up people were 'ignorant but receptive'. Unquestionably Puritan 'lecturers' and itinerant preachers adapted their art to a very wide audience, as did the Salvationists and Hot Gospellers of later times: Richard Baxter described how in Derby 'amongst a poor, tractable people, lately famous for drunkenness' the monthly 'lectures' were crowded out. Then with the break-

The Orthodox true Minifter,   the Seducer and falfe Prophet.

Church and Conventicle

down of Anglican discipline and the stimulation provided by self-taught inspired preachers or the chaplains in the Parliamentarian armies questions about the nature of religion came freely to be debated among civilians and soldiers alike. Though nonconformity was thrust underground in the early years of Charles II's reign, a foreign visitor noted how 'the common people enjoy a liberty which is incredible, every man following that religion and those rites which most suit his fancy'. No doubt the commonest religion was always a mixture of superstition and hope, as reflected by Roger Lowe, the Lancashire apprentice when he wrote in 1663: 'I was pensive and sad and went into the town field and prayed to the Lord, and I hope the Lord heard.'

The common man then was not inevitably a Puritan: he did not rush to enlist in the Parliamentarian armies during the civil wars on the ground that he wanted to overthrow the King and the 'papists'. Most rural folk, if they realized what was going on at all, wanted to keep the war out of their own 'countries' —like the so-called 'Clubmen' of Devon and Cornwall. In so far as the poorer men showed enthusiasm for the war it was because they began to aspire to some degree of social improvement, even some millennium upon the earth, as was promised to them by John Lilburne and his Levellers or Gerrard Winstanley and his Diggers. There was an element of machine-wrecking in their hopes: they would have liked to put an end to the apprenticeship laws, to obtain easier access to common land, to win greater freedom of speech and action, to destroy industrial and commercial monopolies. In fact they got little enough out of the civil wars, except new taxes. Excise duties, introduced to pay for the wars, which became permanent afterwards, affected the price of their beer and other necessities. And as Dr Wedgwood observes, 'apart from these hard but regulated exactions, the common man in the small towns, villages, or open country, was subject to a good deal of casual annoyance and plunder'. Food, cattle, and horses were impounded; not only civilians but soldiers were given in payment I.O.U.s that were not always honoured. But there was a long-term aspect to the civil wars. When ordinary men and women saw their betters squabbling and fighting with each other, authority became undermined. That may have accounted for the underswell of discontent, of which we have already spoken, in the later half of the seventeenth century, and also for the permanent breach in the unity of the Christian Church in England.

Further Reading

Maurice Ashley, *The Stuarts in Love* (illustrated), 1963

M. W. Barley, *The English Farmhouse and Cottage* (illustrated), 1961

Thomas Garden Barnes, *Somerset, 1625–1640*, 1961

Elizabeth Burton, *The Jacobeans at Home* (illustrated), 1962

Alice Clark, *Working Life of Women in the 17th Century*, 1919

F. G. Emmison, *Jacobean Household Inventories* (Bedfordshire Historical Record Society), 1938

Reginald Lennard (ed.), *Englishmen at Rest and Play, 1558–1714*, 1931

Eleanor Trotter, *Seventeenth Century Life in a Country Parish*, 1919

C. V. Wedgwood, *The Common Man in the Civil War*, 1957

III

The Middle Classes

At no period in English history, including recent times, has it been possible to define the middle classes with any degree of precision. Terms like the lower or upper middle classes have been loosely used and are hard to measure by any objective standard. Professional classes can be more easily defined, since usually some examination, licence, or discipline has been needed to qualify into them: that was nearly always the case in the Stuart period. The seventeenth century has also been accepted as an age in which the bourgeosie—that is to say an urban business class—was expanding both in England and in France —though in England it was never a really distinctive class. It was also a golden age for the English 'yeomanry', who were to disappear with purely capitalist society and the industrialization of England, and who may reasonably be thought of as the rural middle class.

THE YEOMANRY

In this age importance attached to the idea of 'status' or 'degree' and the term yeoman was commonly used in legal and other documents to denote the status above that of the 'husbandman' and below that of the 'gentleman'. Yeomen either sprang from old free-tenant families long settled on the lands of their fathers or made their way up. Though they sometimes supplemented their incomes in other ways and aimed to collect a stock of money and implements—they have been called ambitious small capitalists—in essence they were hard-working farmers. The typical yeoman was a modest freeholder cultivating his own land, usually a few hundred acres of arable and pasture; but the term also included tenants on copyholds or similar lease, that is to say with a lengthy security of tenure. The distinction between the yeoman and the husbandman may simply have been in the average size of their holdings, for the husbandman was sometimes described as a 'petty farmer' or 'meaner farmer'. The sons of yeomen were often reckoned to be husbandmen.

The number of yeomen in Stuart England has been variously estimated at between 70,000 and over 200,000, but their importance in the community outweighed their numbers. Their yearly income ranged between £40 and £200 a year, but the amount of capital they acquired varied. Some yeomen left over £500 worth of goods to their families, others as little as £15 or £20. Their farmhouses might contain as many as eight or ten rooms. Frequently they were able to extend their premises by adding new buildings or outhouses and accumulating more

A yeoman's farmhouse

furniture and implements. Some of their houses had windows with glass in them and chimneys to carry away the smoke from their log fires. Most of these farmhouses were built of plaster and timber with thatched roofs, but good use was made of local stone. Devonshire yeomen lived in 'cob' houses, cob being a mixture of mud, straw, chalk, gravel, and slate. In the north of England, in the Cotswolds, and Cornwall stone was more commonly employed for domestic building.

The yeoman farmer put back the profits he obtained from his crops or sheep or from selling cattle and such side-lines as weaving and the like into his farm, fields, and stock. He had a reputation for being careful rather than extravagant. Thus he might be able to improve his economic position. Robert Furze, a Devonshire yeoman said of another yeoman and his wife: 'When this John and Mary were first married, they had but little, but God did so prosper them that before she died they had 400 bullocks and great store of money and other such stuff and were as well furnished of all things in their house as any one man of their degree was in all their country.' They owed their progress to sheer slogging work. Most of them toiled so hard

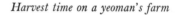

Harvest time on a yeoman's farm

that they had little time for recreation; but they enjoyed bowls and cards or a game of shuffleboard. They got the best out of their servants and apprentices, and in this respect contemporary writers contrasted them with gentlemen farmers.

Making cheese

The yeoman's wife was expected to play her full part. The yeoman was generous over weddings and funerals, but he got excellent value out of his family and relatives. Much spinning and weaving were done in yeomen's homes in the clothing counties. The wives made butter, cheese, jam, and preserves and kept a good table. Yeomen were very hospitable and judging from the number of plates recorded in inventories held large parties. The wives were experts in herbs and acted as the family's doctor. The Reverend Richard Baxter, himself a yeoman's son, thought that the yeomen's wives overdid the housework and were unduly fastidious.

Most yeomen were pretty well educated. They learned their letters at the petty schools in the villages or on their own family hearths; they attended the free grammar schools; many of them went to universities; some of their sons became clergymen. They read the bible and other religious books; sometimes they had modest libraries. They left money to further education.

It was often maintained that the yeomen furnished the real strength and defence of the English nation; they manned the militia at times of crisis; more important, they furnished much of the staff of rural government. Sometimes they acted as constables, occasionally as churchwardens, but invariably they were to be found on the middle rungs of the local administrative ladder, as overseers of the poor, surveyors of the highways, bridgewardens and the like. These were unenviable jobs. The care of the highways, as distinct from the by-roads, and bridges was the responsibility of the parish, but the rich tried to escape their obligations and the poor evaded their work. Often these officials, who were unpaid, had to go to the justices to see that the work was done under threat of fines. During the period of Puritan supremacy yeomen came into their own. For example, they must have been delighted when they were able to fine Lieutenant-General Thomas Fairfax for patronizing a stage show and use the money to spend on the poor.

Undoubtedly Puritan teaching appealed strongly to the yeoman class: its emphasis on the idea of work as a calling from God attracted them. It is known that a number of leading Puritan preachers were the sons of yeomen; so were some of the early Quakers and the nonconformists who migrated to New England. But others were Anglicans or Roman Catholics. One yeoman said of another that 'his religion was part of his copyhold which he takes from his landlord, and refers it wholly to his discretion'. But most hard-working yeomen must surely have resented the lazy, unambitious, careless life of many of their betters; and understandably more yeomen fought on the Parliamentarian side in the civil wars than for the Royalists.

MERCHANTS

The existence of a mercantile community stretches far back into English history: in the middle ages the Merchant Staplers, who sold wool abroad, and the Merchant Adventurers, who were concerned mainly with cloth, dominated the export trade. But in Elizabethan and Stuart times all kinds of trading expanded both at home and abroad. Thomas Mun wrote his celebrated book significantly called *England's Treasure by Foreign Trade*. Henry Robinson, another economic pamphleteer, son of a London mercer, writing in 1641, spoke of inland merchants, exporters and importers, and merchants concentrating on re-exports. But these divisions were not rigid. For example, there were merchant shopkeepers, while yeomen often engaged in trade, though neither of these combinations was strictly legal. Nor were exporters necessarily specialists. Merchants who

The Royal Exchange, as rebuilt after the Fire of London

shipped cloth abroad took imports in exchange and disposed of them at home. In the reign of Charles II over 3,000 merchants operated on the Royal Exchange in London, and of these nearly two thirds were engaged in foreign trade. Many merchants too were found outside London. In Norwich at the start of the century, according to Sir Thomas Wilson, there were 24 aldermen each worth £20,000. Bristol, Newcastle, and many of the outports boasted merchant adventurers. But in the capital itself men rose to become millionaires in modern terms.

Industry and shipping flourished during the Stuart period, but foreign trade advanced most rapidly of all. It has been estimated that the value of English cloth exports rose threefold by the reign of Queen Anne, as compared with a century before; and though the demand for the rougher cloths declined somewhat, the so-called 'new draperies' were selling well. Like the yeoman class, most merchants ploughed their profits back into their own businesses until they had made a pile. Then they launched out into other ventures, for they did not cease to be enterprising. We may mention four merchants of whom we know something. Thomas Cullum, son of a yeoman, was apprenticed by his father to a city draper in 1607; by the time he had completed his indentures he had a capital of less than £100 (later he inherited another £200 from his father). After staying with his master for another five years, he had accumulated nearly £1,000. Then he entered into a partner-

Sir Lionel Cranfield, Earl of Middlesex (1575–1645)

ship with his former master and married wisely; by the eve of the civil war he was worth £20,000, mainly gained from the profits of selling cloth. It was not until he was in his fifties that he began dabbling in stocks and buying up London property. He was able to provide portions of £2,000 each for his daughters and died worth about £50,000.

Yet that was a modest success story compared with those of Sir Lionel Cranfield and Sir John Banks. Cranfield, born in 1575, was apprenticed at the age of 15 to a member of the Grocers Company. After seven years he was able to set up on his own, with the aid of a small legacy, and to marry his master's daughter. In due course he was buying cloth from 79 different sources in the west of England and 28 in Yorkshire, and did a roaring export business in good cloth with the Netherlands and rougher cloth with Germany, to the value of at least £16,000 a year. Once he had amassed sufficient capital, he widened his interests by buying land, by farming taxes, by lending money, and by speculating. Before he was 30 he could afford to take offices in the royal service, and eventually became Lord Treasurer of England with the title of Earl of Middlesex. In the end he was disgraced for alleged peculation; but he seems to have been worth £100,000 when he died.

John Banks, born nearly 40 years later, had the advantage of being a son of a tradesman and draper in Kent who left him some capital. He did extremely well out of foreign trading, doubling his capital in six years; then he started lending large sums of money at ten per cent (six per cent, the official rate, plus four per cent 'gratuity'); he advanced money to the Royal Navy on equally profitable terms; he bought a good deal of land in Kent. At 50 he was worth £100,000 and when he died he was said to have been worth £200,000—a multi-millionaire by present standards.

Lastly we may consider another less successful merchant, Thomas Papillon: son of French father and Italian mother, he was born in Putney in 1623 and was apprenticed at the age of 14 to a London merchant who had married one of his cousins. He started trading on his own account before he completed his apprenticeship and during the civil war did business with Oliver Cromwell; though himself a Royalist in sympathies, he was concerned in attempts to reconcile Parliament and the Roundhead Army in 1647. His French connections helped him to trade with France, notably as an importer of wine and brandy, but he also rose to be a Deputy Governor of the East India Company, a contractor for victualling the navy, and a landowner in Kent. He was a public-spirited man who left legacies to the Mercers Company, Christ's Hospital, and the poor of the French Church in London.

There were many big names among the merchants of the Stuart age: Sir Martin Noell, the friend of Oliver Cromwell, who dabbled in tax farming as well as commerce, but went bankrupt under Charles II; Sir Josiah Child, the great East India merchant and pioneer banker; Sir John Winter, an early arms manufacturer, and so on. To become apprentices to men like these would cost as much as £400 to £600; but it would have been worth it. Many of these merchants set up as financiers, such as Papillon's close friend, Michael Godfrey, who became Deputy Governor of the Bank of England and was killed while talking to King William III. Though some of them had substantial industrial interests, they made most of their money by trade. This was more especially the case at the start of the Stuart era; the late Professor Tawney wrote: 'Commerce, not manufactures or mining, if territorial wealth be excepted, yielded the great fortunes.' Commerce later provided capital for investments of all kinds; commerce dominated City politics; and, in the end, com-

A merchant's wife

47

merce mixed on almost equal terms with the landed aristocracy.

But while it is true that the big merchants to some extent intermarried with the landed gentry and even the aristocracy both in the reigns of King Charles I and King Charles II, the commercial classes were pretty closely knit. It was usual for merchants and industrialists, big or small, to marry the daughters of their confrères. Papillon, for instance, was linked with Burlamachi, who was a big financier, as well as with the Godfreys; Banks married a daughter of Sir John Dethick, another big City financier. Thomas Cullum married a daughter of Nicholas Crisp, a Royalist merchant, famous as a tax farmer. In the City of London most merchants and tradesmen lived over their shops or business premises, and their wives often took an active part in their affairs.

Towards the end of the century Gregory King estimated that there were 2,000 eminent merchants and 8,000 lesser merchants in the kingdom, as well as 50,000 'shopkeepers and tradesmen'. Merchants were a broad category, ranging from the immensely wealthy Cranfield or Banks down to the modest shopkeeper or retailer who cried his wares on London Bridge and might die worth no more than £30. But the expansion of English shipping and colonies stimulated by wars against the Dutch and French brought an all-round increase in wealth, even in the once depressed cloth industry; foreign trade spread from its old markets in northern and central Europe southwards to the Mediterranean: trade with Spain, Portugal, and Italy increased and more exports flowed in from the Near East and India.

In the reign of Charles II a new gospel was being preached.

Shopkeepers and tradesmen

'Trade', said Roger Coke in 1671, 'is now become the lady which in the present age is more courted and celebrated than in any former by all the princes and politicians of the world.' 'The whole world', declared Dudley North, himself a successful merchant, 'as to trade is but one nation or people.' Whereas at the outset of the seventeenth century the big 'landed' and 'moneyed' interests were still distinct, after the Stuart restoration they were increasingly mixed. In fact in the reign of Queen Anne England was already entitled to call itself a nation of shopkeepers. By 1728 Daniel Defoe was able to write: 'An Estate is but a Pond, but Trade is a Spring.'

THE PROFESSIONS

In Stuart England, wrote one of its most famous historians, Sir George Clark, the members of the middle classes became more numerous:

> The rewards of success became greater for them; their functions became more specialized. New types of middle class men emerged such as paid scientists, and journalists. In the City the occupations of dealers in money were divided and subdivided. There were accountants most of whom taught accountancy as well as keeping books for their clients. . . . The army was virtually a new profession. . . . The vertical division between business and the professions became clearer, but at the same time the professions became more hierarchical. . . .

In fact throughout this age can be seen a gradual decline in amateur status. In the opening of the period one obtains the impression that anyone might set up as a country doctor or solicitor. An ambitious young man with some sort of 'pull' might buy himself a post in the royal administration. Most of the officers who served in the civil wars were amateurs. Courtiers, like the first Duke of Buckingham, would offer to take command at sea with the greatest equanimity, and this tradition persisted until the reign of William and Mary.

But gradually more professionalism came in: doctors were expected to pass examinations; naval officers were required to have been at sea; and so on. As will be seen later, the universities of Oxford and Cambridge were ceasing to be purely ecclesiastical seminaries catering roughly for what may be called the lower middle classes and were thrown open to the sons of gentlemen who needed a higher education in order to enter professions other than the Church. 'Men who wished to enter the old and new professions', it has been observed, 'streamed through the university gates.' The same writer, Dr David Mathew, has suggested that while the squires, both great and small, put their children into the law and foreign service, the yeomen and 'lower burgess grouping . . . had seeped into medicine and teaching and had coloured the large mass of the clergy'. At any rate there can hardly be any question that a large professional class of men who relied for the bulk of their incomes on fees, salaries, and the perquisites of offices and not on rents or investments came to the front in the Stuart age.

LAWYERS

The law was one of the oldest professions, but now it was becoming more specialized; not only were barristers differentiated from attorneys, but also attorneys from solicitors. The four Inns of Court and two Inns of Chancery still afforded a finishing school for a vast number of gentlemen who had no intention of practising at the Bar; but those who wanted to become barristers had to go through a long period of training even after first attending a university. Study at the London Inns was the road not merely to a well-paid professional career but also to some lucrative offices—in an earlier age Sir Nicholas Bacon, the lawyer who was the father of Francis Bacon, made about £2,000 a year while he held office in the Court of Augmentations and the Court of Wards. It was also an excellent entry into politics. In the parliament of 1614 there were 48 professional lawyers, as compared with 42 merchants, and in the Long Parliament of 1640 75 barristers, as compared with 70 merchants and speculators: in fact they were the largest group after the landed gentry in the House of Commons.

This was both an incredibly litigious age and also a criminal one. The law was complicated. The boundaries between the common law and the chancery law were not at all clearly drawn; in addition work was to be had in the admiralty courts and in the ecclesiastical courts subject to the civil law. Among justices of the peace a sprinkling of trained lawyers, known as the 'quorum' was required. While the expansion of commerce and the interpretation of business contracts swelled the volume of legal business, questions of inheritance, and disputes over real property gave an immense amount of work to lawyers.

Masters of Chancery

Thus though the training was long and expensive, the rewards were rich. One can see that from the career of Francis North, who eventually became Chief Justice of the Common Pleas. After having been a Fellow Commoner of St John's, Cambridge, for two years, he was admitted to the Middle Temple 'into the moiety of a petit chamber which his father bought for him in 1655'. Here he ate his dinners and 'dispatched the greatest part of all the year books' and attended the sessions of the King's Court and Common Pleas as a spectator until he was called to the Bar in 1661. He then 'performed his moots', that is to say did exercises in pleading both in the Inns of Chancery and in his own hall, and eventually started practice in 1663. During these years of preparation his father allowed him £60 a year and he supplemented this by doing odd jobs for solicitors and attorneys. Then he bought himself a chamber 'two pair of stairs high', which was more fashionable than a ground-floor chamber: £300 it cost him for a dark, dismal hole. However, fortunately he was friendly with the son of the then Attorney General; and soon plenty of work came his way, to put him on the path to becoming a justice of assize, Lord Chief Justice, and Lord Keeper.

Not all lawyers shot up like that. Some wasted their time at the Inns; others became teachers of the law; others followed judges on their circuits or practised as qualified clerks. But many, as today, were dependent for a livelihood on friendly solicitors. North, for example, received work from 'Mr Baker, a solicitor in Chancery who for his singular integrity was famous'. But not all solicitors or attorneys were scrupulous. Indeed an Act of James I's reign had vainly attempted to confine the profession to 'those who had been found in their dealings to be of skilful and honest disposition'. Nor for that matter were judges always men of integrity. Traditionally judges were regarded as 'lions under the throne'. Frequently therefore they gave their decisions under pressure from the monarch. An age that boasted a judge like George Jeffreys, whose bullying of witnesses and prisoners in the interests of the Crown gave him an eternal notoriety, could surely not be complacent about the rule of law. And in fact in both the high court and in the magistrates' courts class interests coloured decisions. In nine cases out of ten the practice of the law was more profitable to the barristers and solicitors than to the litigant or prisoner.

DOCTORS AND CLERGY

Doctors formed a rising professional class; it was not surprising that they were in demand in view of the many epidemics and scourges that regularly swept the country. Physicians and later surgeons required licences. Physicians were usually university men, though it was recognized that they received a better training at Leiden or Padua than Oxford or Cambridge. Though early in the century William Harvey, physician extraordinary to King Charles I, discovered the circulation of the blood and Sir Theodore Mayerne, another royal doctor, stressed the importance of chemistry, more physicians based

An apothecary's shop

their practices on the classical teachings of Hippocrates and Galen as reverently handed down through the Middle Ages. If they had stuck to Hippocrates' advice about keeping the patient in bed and letting nature take its course, all might have gone better; but too much attention was paid to Galen's doctrine of 'the four humours' between which a balance had to be kept by copious bleedings or enforced vomiting. One extremely successful doctor, Baldwin Hamey the elder, observed that 'all

William Harvey (1578–1657)

patients were the better for evacuants in the early stages of disease and he gave emetics and purgatives, whatever the condition'. However he left clysters to surgeons. For most diseases he thought he had a suitable remedy, provided it was given in large enough doses. But he accepted a high rate of maternal mortality as inevitable and 'looked on the conduct of childbirth as directed by fate rather than the physician'. His son, an even more fashionable doctor in Stuart London, said 'Let blood in cases of great distress until the patient faints', and thought that since the plague had defeated Hippocrates there could be no cure for it. The Hameys were more typical doctors of their age than either Harvey or Mayerne, who fought a rather losing battle against the revolting remedies normally prescribed. Still no doubt the average doctor learned a good deal more from experience than from books.

From itinerant quack to court oculist: Sir William Read treating a patient

Physicians were able to charge high fees and sometimes asked as much as £50 or £100 for a 'guaranteed cure'. Surgeons did even better, though just as physicians had no stethoscopes, surgeons lacked anaesthetics. James Yonge, a Plymouth surgeon, who learned his trade in the navy and also seems to have practised as a physician (his cure for scurvy was to give the patient wild vetches steeped in beer) earned from 25 to 100 guineas for a single operation and boasted that he obtained £120 in one year for treating sailors for the pox (syphilis) in the naval hospital at Plymouth.

Qualified doctors were scarce and so were hospitals. In London there were at first only three, St Bartholomew's, St Thomas's, and the new Bethlehem or Bedlam for mad people. (Hospitals were opened at Chelsea and Greenwich during the late seventeenth century.) In Bedlam Yonge saw 'Cromwell's porter', an old man seven feet six inches tall whose bed was covered with bibles and his breeches filled with them. Owing to the poor condition of most roads, it was often impossible for doctors to visit their patients in time and frequently remedies were prescribed by correspondence. The general scarcity of licensed practitioners and the regular prevalence of diseases from smallpox to tuberculosis meant that a licence to practise was virtually a licence to print money. Certainly men like Baldwin Hamey the younger were able to distribute immense benefactions and still leave adequate fortunes to their families.

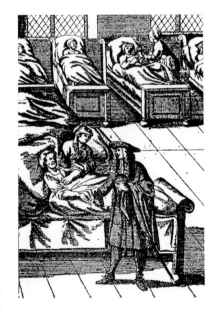

A doctor does his hospital round

If doctoring was a lucrative business, being a clergyman was certainly not, unless one happened to be a bishop. But even bishops were not all that well off. They had been mulcted by Queen Elizabeth I and it was less easy for them to exploit their tenants than for lay landlords. 'Many bishoprics', writes Mr Christopher Hill, 'were seriously impoverished.' For example, in 1649 Durham was carrying a rent charge of over £1,000 a year to the Crown, while earlier Ely had to pay the same sum annually to the Earl of Oxford. Even the archbishopric of Canterbury was worth only about £2,000 a year, out of which a big establishment had to be maintained. It was not a vast income compared with those of the nobility, successful merchants, or other professional men. But at the other end of the scale the ordinary parish clergy, apart from a certain number of rectors, who still received the full benefit of tithes, a tenth of the harvests paid by their parishioners, were little better off than the poorer members of their congregations. Fifty pounds a year was a good stipend for a vicar. On the other hand, they could and did till their own 'glebe' lands, which were sometimes extensive, and supplement their stipends by school-mastering or by pluralism (looking after more than one church). The Reverend Ralph Josselin, an Essex clergyman, for example, made an additional £70 a

A bishop

year by teaching in school and by such side-lines as buying and selling hops, investing in a part-share in a ship, and purchasing a little landed property, built himself up an estate worth nearly £700. In the reign of Charles I one or two clergymen are said to have kept inns: one was caught poaching 'with a hawk upon his fist and speaking to his dogs'. But in spite of the sneers made against them by Puritan propagandists because they could not or did not preach, many Anglican clergy were educated men with university degrees. Undoubtedly the quality of both the higher and the lower clergy was raised considerably during the reign of Charles II. Naturally they were of many types, some who adapted themselves to the changing political winds, others who preferred to give up their livings rather than conform. But most were conscientious exponents of their profession. After their emoluments were improved by the institution of Queen Anne's Bounty in 1704 (a fund to supplement inadequate stipends) the parson came to be accepted as the leading figure in the village community after the squire. And well-to-do gentry did not hesitate to put their younger sons into the Church as being a respected profession.

SERVICES TO THE CROWN

Though convenient, it is inaccurate to speak of professional civil servants in the Stuart period. In the first place, no precise qualifications were required from the servants of the Crown; secondly, no distinction could have been drawn between those who would later have been described as Cabinet Ministers and the heads of departments of state. King Charles II required it to be known that he alone ruled his kingdom and his Ministers did what he ordered them to, like any civil servant in later times. Many members of parliament held offices under the Crown; on the other hand, quite a number of the King's servants turned against their masters, Charles I and James II.

Most of those who served the monarch bought their offices. Such offices were much sought after for various reasons: they gave access to fashionable society; they frequently yielded rich financial benefits to the holders; and they opened the way to higher preferment. It has been said that such appointments were usually made by patrimony or by patronage combined with purchase. What it amounted to, in short, was that an aspiring candidate for public office had to know somebody with influence at Court. Often offices were reversionary in families, but the reversions might be put up for sale. At the bottom of the ladder mere clerkships might not need to be purchased, but most other offices had to be paid for in one way or another. Not much was asked by way of qualification. At the very top office-holders were expected to work hard: one has only to study the official papers of a Strafford, a Danby, or a Godolphin to see that they did. But in the middle range of the royal service routine duties were often put on to deputies while the lucky holders of the office pocketed the profits.

And the profits were often considerable. Salaries might be nominal or negligible, but in most cases there were perquisites, allowances, or gratuities, 'cuts' to be obtained from contractors, fees to be received for licences, and so on. Sometimes office-holders were successfully accused of corruption or peculation —like Francis Bacon—but everybody knew what was going on and took the risk of being caught or framed by a political enemy.

In any case the line between what was and was not legitimate was blurred.

One cannot generalize about how competent, conscientious, or efficient a professional 'civil servant' then was. How far was Samuel Pepys, the navy commissioner, typical? We know well from reading his celebrated diary that, once he settled down, he became diligent and effective, working

Samuel Pepys (1633–1703)

from early in the morning until late at night, mastering the technicalities of his job by consulting experts, organizing his office efficiently, and taking wise decisions in times of crisis. On the other hand, as Dr Aylmer writes, 'we may think of the Clerk of the Ordnance [in Charles I's reign] being found making a bonfire of departmental records in order to escape the scrutiny of an investigating committee' or 'officers of the [Royal] Household systematically cheating the Crown for forty years by means of a transparent and shameless accounting device'. Though there may have been loyal and able bureaucrats, many bought their way into office simply for what they could get out of it, working as little as they need. Men like Sir Arthur Ingram or (in an earlier age) Sir Nicholas Bacon were complete professionals only when it came to lining their own pockets; but the system was so riddled with corruption that it was a wonder that government functioned at all.

The Royal Navy offered a genuine professional service, because it had existed so long and was so important to the nation's security. In it were to be found those who were called 'tarpaulin captains', that is to say men who were experienced seamen, having learned their trade in the merchant navy, and gentleman officers, who received their commissions through influence at Court. By the end of the Stuart period the payment of officers was being placed on a more regular basis. From 1653 captains of first-rate warships like the *Royal Sovereign* received as much as £21 a month and midshipmen £2 5s. a month and *pari passu* along the scale, together with what might be called 'fringe benefits', such as free treatment in royal hospitals. In the reign of William and Mary naval officers were given half-pay when their ships were out of commission and pensions if they were wounded. Gradually naval officers were subjected to a clearer code of discipline and their professional status emphasized by their being exempted from certain civilian duties. Ordinary seamen, who might have been pressed into the service, were paid 19s. a month, with all found. Though men like General George Monk and Prince Rupert might have had little experience (except in gunnery, which was important) before they put to sea as admirals, in the later half of the century most naval officers from King James II downwards were becoming genuinely professional men, and some of them were retained in their posts in spite of changes of their political allegiance during the civil wars.

If the army had not yet acquired such a professional tradition as the navy it was because until 1660 a professional or standing army did not exist. James I and Charles I found difficulty in raising a fighting force because the militia or 'citizen army', though reasonably well armed, was virtually untrained outside

Life aboard the Royal Sovereign

the City of London, and then had to be recruited and not pressed. During the civil wars officers and troopers were quite well paid—though ordinary infantrymen only received 8*d*. or 9*d*. a day. In the reign of Charles II troopers were paid 2*s*. 6*d*. a day and foot soldiers a shilling.

The practice which prevailed during the civil wars remained unchanged by the reign of Queen Anne whereby colonels raised their own regiments, having paid for their commissions, and took what profit they could out of running them. Indeed the method of collecting taxes or running royal services on the basis of 'farming' out or 'commissioning' was fundamental to the age and opened the way to fraud and blackmail. Yet contemporaries did not think of such methods as being in themselves abuses. When the first Duke of Marlborough, one of the greatest of English generals, built himself a fortune out of his various posts and by taking commissions from army contractors, they did not in the least detract from his professional efficiency—he would have claimed that he earned every penny. Thus in the British army—which became a permanent force with the establishment of the Grenadier Guards, the Coldstream Guards, and the Royal Horse Guards about the time of the Restoration—a professional tradition was being decisively established in the Stuart era.

An infantry officer

Further Reading

Maurice Ashley, *Financial and Commercial Policy under the Cromwellian Protectorate*, 1962

G. E. Aylmer, *The King's Servants*, 1961

Mildred Campbell, *The English Yeoman*, 1960

G. N. Clark, *Aspects of Stuart England*, 1960

F. J. Fisher (ed.), *Essays in the Economic and Social History of Tudor and Stuart England*, 1960

Christopher Hill, *Economic Problems of the Church*, 1956

John Keevil, *Hamey the Stranger* (illustrated), 1952
— —, *The Stranger's Son* (illustrated), 1953
Geoffrey Keynes, *The Life of William Harvey* (illustrated), 1966
F. N. L. Poynter (ed.), *The Journal of James Yonge* (illustrated), 1963
Alan Simpson, *The Wealth of the Gentry, 1540–1660*, 1961
R. H. Tawney, *Business and Politics under James I*, 1958

IV

The Nobility and Gentry

'The nobility and chief gentry of England', wrote Edward Chamberlayne in 1674, 'have been even by strangers compared to the finest flower [flour], but the lowest sort of common people to the coarsest bran.' Their 'sparkle', their 'port', their 'hospitality' were much admired. Throughout the Stuart age they remained, under the monarch, the most eminent figures in English life. It is true that the old peerage had suffered a set-back when the Tudors reigned. Some aristocratic families had been virtually wiped out in the Wars of the Roses; others had been severely treated by Henry VII and Henry VIII. In the early years of Queen Elizabeth I there remained only one duke in England, the Duke of Norfolk, and he perished on the scaffold for treason. Altogether 62 titled families had existed at the outset of the reign of Queen Elizabeth, of which 22 were extinct by 1640.

But the Stuarts created peers with lavish hands. 'I can make a peer,' said the first of them cynically, 'but I cannot make a gentleman.' Soon there were plenty of dukes. King James I made his favourite George Villiers Duke of Buckingham (as in Scotland he had made another favourite Duke of Lennox). Then Charles II's illegitimate sons were created dukes: the Duke of Monmouth (his son by Lucy Walter), the Duke of Southampton, the Duke of Grafton, and the Duke of Northumberland (his sons by Barbara Palmer), the Duke of St Albans (his son by Nell Gwyn) and the Duke of Richmond (by Louise de Kéroualle). Serviceable politicians could count on obtaining earldoms: Sir Robert Cecil became Earl of Salisbury, Lionel

Peers of the realm: earls

Cranfield the merchant became Earl of Middlesex, Sir Edward Hyde Earl of Clarendon, Sir Thomas Osborne Earl of Danby, and later Duke of Leeds, George Savile, Earl and then Marquess of Halifax, and Sidney Godolphin Earl of Godolphin, and so on. While Queen Anne's favourite adviser, Robert Harley, received the earldom of Oxford, Henry St John, who tried to supplant him, was very angry indeed because the Queen refused him an earldom.

Thus only a few of the peers could claim to be of ancient lineage; most of them could trace a respectable ancestry only as far back as the Reformation; some were mere upstarts, gilded officials. But it was accepted that peers, once created, had to be provided with the means to support their position and prestige. Both King James I and his Minister, Cecil, were concerned that this should be arranged. So they were granted Crown lands at nominal rents or given sinecures, patents, and monopolies: a few actually received large gratuities from the Treasury. They also sometimes condescended to marry, or marry their sons, into families with fortunes from business. At one time it used to be thought that the economic position of the peerage had declined relatively to the rest of the landed gentry before and after the civil wars; but recent research does not bear this out. One or two peers might have been ruined by gross extravagance, for example, the 'splendid spendthrift', the Earl of Cleveland. But most of them did not worry much over their expenditure. To give one example, the Earl of Bedford spent over £1,500 simply on the cost of his clothes and those of his attendants when they all appeared at the coronation of Charles II. The peerage was nearly always able to recoup its fortunes, even after the confiscations of Royalists' properties during the civil wars. The first Lord Fitzwilliam ran up a debt of £20,000, but his son and heir was able to make a triumphant recovery by marrying the daughter of a Lord Mayor of London. The incomes from land of peers in the reign of Charles I averaged £10,000 a year and three of them, the Earls of Worcester, Newcastle, and Shrewsbury had incomes of £20,000, and that was apart from what they obtained from offices and investments. After the restoration of Charles II the nobility steamed ahead. The Earls of Bedford doubled their money in 30 years. The Earl of Bridgwater is said to have netted over £700,000 out of his appointment as Paymaster to Marlborough's army.

Most of the nobility lived at a prodigiously high rate, owning several houses and having many dependants and servants. Robert Cecil, Earl of Salisbury, who at one stage had £20,000 of free capital to invest, mostly the perquisites of offices, built himself Hatfield House in four years, Cranborne in Dorset, Salisbury House in the Strand, and a house at Chelsea; he had inherited three other large houses from his father. The landed nobility kept little courts of their own, travelled about the country in glittering cavalcades, entertaining kings and queens on a grand scale, bought jewels, pictures, sculpture; they hunted over vast parklands and spent huge sums on food, drink, and clothing.

A party at the Duke of Newcastle's house

A London Residence: Montagu House, rebuilt in 1687

Roger North described in detail what it was like to stay with the Duke and Duchess of Beaufort at Badminton near Bristol in the reign of Charles II. The Duke had 'above £2,000 per annum in his hands which he managed by stewards, bailiffs, and servants', he bred all his horses, and he 'had two hundred persons in his family all provided for'; and 'in his capital house nine original tables covered every day'. 'All the provisions of the family came from foreign parts as merchandise', but soap, candles, and ale were manufactured on the premises. The stables would accommodate many strings of horses. Suitors for the Duke's favours were put up at a nominal charge in a private inn.

'As for the duke and duchess', added North, 'and their friends, there was no time of the day without diversion. Breakfast in her gallery that opened into the gardens; then, perhaps, a deer was to be killed, or the gardens, and parks with the several sorts of deer, to be visited; and if required mounting, horses of the duke's were brought for all the company. . . .' The gentlemen would be invited down to the vaults 'which were very large and sumptuous' to take wine. And the Duke 'always had some new project of building, walling, or planting, which he would show and ask his friends their advice about'.

Salisbury's estate at Theobalds so impressed the once

penurious James I that he got him to exchange it for Crown property at Hatfield. The great house had magnificent mullioned windows, square towers, each with four turrets surmounted by a golden lion, and a fountain court containing a kind of planetarium. Hatfield House, which Cecil built on the estate he exchanged for Theobalds, the site of an old palace, was an equally fantastic creation with a most elaborate centrepiece half-tower, half-gateway with double columns carrying each storey and behind all that a complicated clock tower. Sometimes the nobility built themselves houses in which they could not hope to live for long. The first Duke of Devonshire took 18 years to rebuild Chatsworth in Derbyshire and died in the year it was finished; the first Duke of Marlborough did not see the completion of Blenheim Palace; it took the Duke of Bridgwater many years to finish his Palladian palace at Cannons, an estate that he purchased in 1713. The leading nobility expected to serve on the Privy Council and most Ministers of State were peers. It was not until the days of Sir Robert Walpole that any leading politician stayed for any length of time a member of

Chatsworth, Derbyshire: the seat of the Duke of Devonshire, built 1687–1705

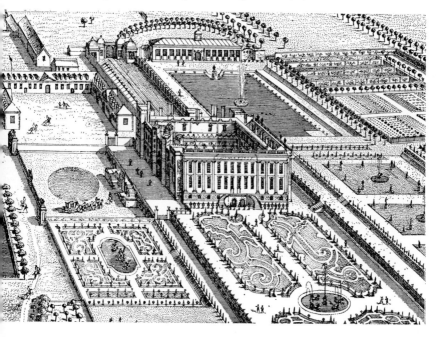

Robert Carr and Frances Howard, Earl and Countess of Somerset

the House of Commons. (One excepts of course the Cromwellian period, but even Cromwell recreated an Upper House.) The nobility had many privileges and exemptions; they often did not pay debts to their tradesmen and they did not expect to be sued. Indeed it was claimed in a case brought before the Star Chamber that noblemen and women were privileged from arrest. At any rate the royal Court was barred to bailiffs. According to Mr Ogg, since a peer who committed a criminal offence might demand to be tried by his peers and, even if convicted, might expect royal clemency, 'there was a reasonable chance that, after two murders, he would remain unhanged'. Certainly Robert Carr, Earl of Somerset, and Frances Howard got off lightly after they had both been found guilty of murder by poisoning.

What did the nobility offer the community in return for all their perquisites, privileges, and exemptions? Apart from serving as Ministers and in the Privy Council and holding such Court offices as Lord Steward or Master of the Horse, they were members of the upper house of parliament, they acted as lords lieutenant in the counties, and as chancellors of universities, and in similar posts. How far they performed their functions adequately has been disputed. An American historian has said of the nobles that attended Court in the reign of James I: 'a more unsavoury lot it is hard to come upon in the annals of England'. They are described as having been absurdly extravagant and having gambled and drunk to excess. Their attendance at the House of Lords was by no means regular Though peers frequently accepted the lord lieutenancy of more than one county, this was done for reasons of power and prestige rather than out of a genuine sense of public responsibility.

All this is true up to a point. Certainly some lords lieutenant, the Herberts, for example, spent little time in their counties, and their principal duty, the organization of the militia, was left to their deputies, who themselves were often minor peers; but others, like the Stanleys in Lancashire, played a prominent part in the life of their counties. Unquestionably the political peers, such as Salisbury, Clarendon, Danby, Godolphin, all served the Stuarts with devotion and a high degree of skill, and though they may have made ample money out of their offices, they obtained little by way of

Gambling at dice

gratitude from their royal masters or mistresses. Other peers, like the first Duke of Newcastle, who held no principal office of state, yet had a notable sense of responsibility and used his patronage with discrimination. Indeed Professor Stone writes: 'what distinguished the English aristocracy of this period from the *élites* of other times and places is the relative

Peers and gentry on the Council of War, 1623–4

moderation of their appetites for wealth and power, and the relative sense of social responsibility displayed by some of its members.'

THE PLACE OF THE GENTRY

'Peers and gentry', wrote Mr Hugh Trevor-Roper in a famous essay, 'had, on their different levels, the same problems, the same ambitions, the same conventions, the same tastes. Both were landlords; both had large families; both accepted the rule of primogeniture and the custom of entail; both had to find portions for daughters and younger sons. They built—according to their capacity—similar houses; they were buried in similar tombs. It was an aristocratic age, and the gentry accepted—in general—the standards of value and the conduct of the aristocracy.' If the lay peers furnished the membership of the House of Lords, apart from the bishops, the gentry were overwhelmingly represented in the House of Commons. If the peers were lords lieutenant, deputy lieutenants, or the Custodes Rotulorum at the quarter sessions, the gentry were sheriffs, justices of the peace, and churchwardens. The squires, who gathered at the county quarter sessions or served on the committees during the civil wars, directed, supervised, and organized practically every aspect of rural life. If there were extravagant, vicious, or careless peers, so there were a number of pleasure-loving, decadent, or irresponsible gentry. But like the peers, the gentry as a class held their own throughout the whole of the Stuart period. They profited from bigger rents; they took advantage of boom periods when the price of sheep or crops rose; in the reign of Charles II wheat prices were protected for their benefit; their representatives in the Commons ensured that taxes were kept low to their advantage. Though it was sometimes claimed by contemporaries that the commercial classes were beginning to oust the landed gentry, in fact the two classes inter-

A baronet

68

mingled; many a landlord saved his estates from ruin by a judicious marriage.

The English gentry—defined so far as degree was concerned by the right to put knight, esquire, or gentleman after their names—and to bear a coat of arms—covered a very wide class so far as incomes went. Some of them, like Sir John Spencer, the great moneylender, Sir Giles Mompesson, a notorious monopolist, or Sir Arthur Ingram and Sir Nicholas Crisp made their money out of buying Court offices or engaging in contracting and public finance. Others like the Ishams and Brudenells in Northamptonshire were wool-dealers, sheep farmers, or astute enclosers and improvers, who knew how to make the most out of their inherited estates.

A gentlewoman

Others were modest or even declining gentry, such as the Cromwells of Huntingdonshire, who were simply farmers a little above the level of yeomen, but who had inherited a position in their counties that they felt bound to keep up and could not manage to be so economical as their inferiors. Some managed to live lazily on their rents. On the whole, the economic conditions during the reigns of the first two Stuarts were favourable to the landowning class. Food prices were rising, wages were low, there was a steady demand for wheat, timber and stock. Rents rose and caught up or overhauled prices. There are many instances of families who doubled, trebled, or quadrupled their incomes from land. The structure of the English property law helped to preserve large holdings intact—notably the custom of primogeniture, the laws of entail, the strict settlements arranged by fathers of families, the intermarriages between the well-to-do. Many of their estates had been extended by the purchase of Crown and Church lands during the century following the English Reformation.

These new large landowners who, as Sir Thomas Wilson pointed out, were at the beginning of the seventeenth century

A card party

taking the management of their properties directly into their own hands, as leaseholds fell in, employing capable bailiffs, stewards, and attorneys to advise them, enclosing and improving wherever they could, earned rich rewards. Such men might build up incomes both from rents and from the sales of their produce, to from £1,000 and £5,000 or more a year—and of course when they reached the top level they could consider buying their way into the English, Scottish, or Irish peerages, if they wished, as General Sir Thomas Fairfax's grandfather had done. But below them was a whole range of lesser gentry without access to the Court, who might get into the clutches of moneylenders, who had no liquid capital of any kind, yet insisted on living the high life appropriate to their status. Such men had to be hard-working and energetic indeed to profit at all from the price revolution and the favourable conditions of the markets. Though some gentry may have lost ground, of the general expansion or 'rise' of the gentry in the first half of the Stuart period there can be no question whatever. But they did not necessarily rise at anyone else's expense. Some yeomen became gentry and some gentry were ennobled.

THE DUTIES OF THE GENTRY

It is not too much to say that the justices of the peace were the men who determined the articulation of English life in the Stuart period, and outside the towns they were invariably gentry.

70

The qualifications of a justice of the peace were that he should be of good moral and religious character and own land worth £20 a year. He received no pay for his work other than 4s. a day for attending quarter sessions. Yet to be on the commission of peace carried social prestige: to be excluded from it meant a loss both of power and of influence. When justices of peace were originally established in the fourteenth century only a few were named in each county and their duty was to help administer the law. But during the sixteenth century many fresh obligations were laid upon them and their numbers were materially increased. They were appointed by the Lord Chancellor or Lord Keeper; but in practice when choosing magistrates he took the advice of the lord lieutenant of the county, usually a peer to be found about the Court, or of other local magnates. In fact the lists of J.P.s in a county comprised the roll of nearly all the wealthy and important gentry there. They usually numbered between 40 and 70; in Somerset over 100 names were counted in the 15 years up to 1640. Some of the J.P.s were supposed to be trained lawyers; in effect it sufficed for them to have attended the Inns of Court for a year or two. That was why most established gentry sent their sons to the London Inns, even if they had also been to a university, in order that they might be fitted to become county magistrates.

The justices of the peace exercised control over most other county officials except the lords lieutenant, who were the king's personal representatives. The powers of the sheriff had been reduced since the middle ages: the sheriff could not be a member of parliament or a magistrate, but his duties were to act as the executive officer at the assize court, to see that the arrangements for the meetings of quarter sessions were properly made, and to conduct county elections and supervise the collection of royal revenues. The sheriff, however, was only an annual appointment and, apart from the elections, he generally left the rest of his work to deputies. The magistrates had pretty full control over the high constables and through them the village constables. Indeed by an Act of Charles II the justices became directly responsible for the appointment of all constables. As we have seen, the village constable was the ultimate link in the chain of government and the justices depended on him to carry out their orders and decisions.

Quarter sessions, held in the most important county towns, usually lasted three or four days and their efficiency depended on the clerk of the peace, a paid and usually competent official. The quarter sessions were the great occasion in county life (apart from the occasional visits of the judges of assize, which the magistrates attended). Here the administrative work of the county and many matters were co-ordinated and settled by amicable discussion. It was also a notable social occasion, at any rate when the towns boasted attractive inns and other amenities. In addition, at any rate after 1630, there were petty sessions at which the county magistrates considered with their various officers problems of local government and administration, particularly the relief of the poor.

The magistrates had both legal and administrative duties to perform. Pairs of magistrates might deal with minor misdemeanours, such as petty larceny, but grand larceny and rioting were always left to quarter sessions, and murder and rape were referred to the justices of assize. The administrative responsibilities of the justices of the peace were numerous. William Lambard, the author of *Eirenarcha* (1619), a book for magistrates, wondered how many justices were necessary 'to bear so many, not loads, but stacks of statutes' laid upon them since Henry VII's reign. For they were responsible for

A baronet helps to relieve the poor of the parish

the functioning of the poor laws, for statutes of labourers, for fixing of prices as well as wages, for the licensing of alehouses, for the bastardy laws, for the building and repair of roads and bridges, for matters of public health, and the enrolment of sales of land. Over and above all this they might receive specific instructions from the Privy Council. Though the justices of the assize and the lords lieutenant might be grander people and able to wield greater power, the justices of the peace, especially when they gathered together at the quarter sessions, were reckoned to be the most capable of ensuring the success or failure of public administration.

How conscientious were they? Naturally that depended on the individual. But historians who have examined the records of quarter sessions in different parts of the country are for the most part of the opinion that the active J.P.s did an honest job. Certainly they could find plenty to do, together with looking after their own estates. No doubt the Yorkshire knight, Sir John Reresby, was fairly typical. In his autobiography he wrote how, in 1673, 'I continued this year to build the park wall as I enlarged it and living the most part at Thriberge applied myself to the study and exercise of the office of magistrate of the peace and had so much work that my clerk confessed he made above £40 that year (in fees) out of his place.'

Apart from the magistracy, the sheriffdom, the deputy lieutenancies, and the churchwardenships in the parishes, the country gentlemen furnished most of the members of parliament in the boroughs as well as the shires. To be the premier knight of the shire was the greatest honour to which a gentleman might aspire, apart from a peerage. In each county there were usually one or two families who expected their members to enter parliament, if they wished, and at any rate until the latter part of the reign of Charles II, when a rudimentary party organization was being started, it was a question of jockeying for place. Even in the famous Long Parliament of 1640 that finally overthrew the monarchy the members were not originally divided along party lines: indeed, in theory, party divisions were still thought to be improper. And even after parties came into being the great county families still regularly continued to supply the bulk of the members of parliament right up to the early twentieth century. Until then, of course, like the magistrates, members were unpaid. In the Stuart period typical ruling families were the Weldons in Kent, the Pouletts or Phelipps in Somerset, the Barringtons in Essex, the Montagus in Huntingdonshire, the Stanleys in Lancashire, the Verneys in Buckinghamshire, the Lukes in Bedfordshire, the Grenvilles in Cornwall or the Herberts in Wiltshire. In the Long Parliament three out of five members were 'country gentlemen who lived out of London most of the time, took an active part in the life of their shires, and drew their incomes chiefly, if not solely, from lands'. They were in general, 'country gentry', not 'local gentry', men with property in more than one parish, not mere lords of a single manor. If they are regarded, as they should be, as ambassadors of the localities where they normally themselves held sway, then it might reasonably be claimed that a thousand or more country gentlemen (for they cannot be separated from the peerage, to who many of them were related) were the real rulers of England.

HOMES AND RECREATIONS

The gentry, like the nobility, devoted close attention to improving and beautifying their homes. Though they might rent town houses for a season, what they liked best was to decorate or add to their ancestral residences and not infrequently, when they could afford it, they would build themselves new ones. In the early part of the Stuart period domestic architecture continued in the Elizabethan tradition, E-shaped or T-shaped and built out of timber and local stone. But later, under Dutch influence brick became very fashionable; the first all-brick house is said to have been built at Leeds in 1628. The Earl of Clarendon's rectangular classical house, designed for him in Piccadilly by Roger Pratt, is said to have set a pattern for domestic building. Dutch and French influences contended for a while. But gradually the square classical style won its way through and became enshrined in what we call Queen Anne architecture. With the cheapening of glass, windows became a

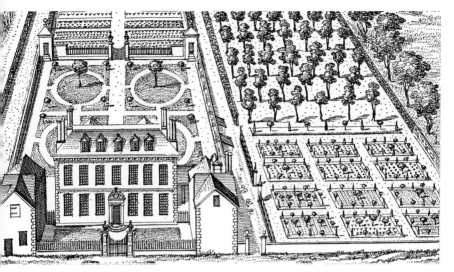

A gentleman's country house and garden

more important feature of a gentleman's house, set in wooden
or stone frames; the sash window was invented and inserted
into a brick façade. A 'hipped' roof, sloping down on all four
sides and a deepening of the rooms from front to back, with the
kitchen thrust well back or down in the house completed the
general difference in style and construction between the houses
that were being built at the close of the Stuart age from the
wide manor houses of Tudor times.

Such houses needed plenty of furniture. It was indeed at first
usual for the nobility and gentry to have heavy and elaborate
chairs and tables, carved chests, Turkey carpets, canopied four-
poster beds; but gradually the age of oak yielded to that of
walnut; more delicate furniture became fashionable; chairs, no
longer luxuries, stools, and cabinets were lighter and more
attractively designed; beds were covered with rich French
brocades. The increase in foreign trade and travel brought
varied ideas from the continental mainland. The predominant
modes were French, but the golden age of English furniture
was approaching.

Gardens were becoming increasingly grandiose parts of a
nobleman's or gentleman's estate. Originally they were con-
ceived in terms of unending and uninspiring geometrical patterns
with tall trees and numerous shrubs. But the flower garden was

becoming more popular and the idea of avenues and gravel paths, of aviaries, beehives and even orangeries were imported from France by such connoisseurs as John Evelyn. Most ladies liked to have herb gardens and orchards to draw upon when planning their gargantuan meals; such vast and varied gardens, of which we have knowledge, were often interspersed with mazes, sundials, and statuary. Tulips and other bulbs were introduced from the Netherlands. In general the gardens of the nobility and gentry remained pretty formal until the eighteenth century.

In these large well-furnished houses and dignified gardens a happy family life as a rule prevailed. It was customary for the nobility and gentry to marry not for love but for estates. (But love often came after marriage: Dorothy Osborne thought, though she herself married for love, that it was all a gamble either way.) Wives brought in useful portions ranging from about £1,000 to £8,000. Armed with these, the newly married man could afford to pay off his debts or improve his own estate and to employ plenty of domestic servants, who were cheap enough. Gentlewomen preferred to be in command of their own homes to sitting about in their father's houses. Children, if they survived the hazards of birth and the risks of the first year or two of life, were brought up by family 'nannies' and amused with balls, drums, dolls, and hobby-horses. Parents, after a while, became less severe in their discipline than in earlier days. James I set a good example of tenderness towards children and Charles I was a model father. Boys were sent to grammar schools at an early age or else had private tutors (the clergy were glad enough of such work), but girls were mostly educated at home, often by their mothers.

The outdoor life was reckoned all-important.

A gentleman and his family

Hunting

It was said that even gentlemen with incomes as low as between £500 and £1,000 a year usually had two or three parks and, like the royalty and nobility, occupied many of their waking hours in hunting. James II was a pioneer of fox-hunting, but before his time stag-hunting, coursing, hawking or shooting sitting-birds were more popular pastimes. Gentlemen's wives, when they were not actually bearing children—they might have eight, ten, or even 12, of whom half would survive with luck—spent much of their time in their gardens growing flowers or herbs or fruit that was principally used for making preserves and pies rather than eaten raw. Tennis (that is to say 'real tennis') was a popular game among gentlemen, Charles II being an enthusiastic player—so was croquet or 'pel-mel'—but team sports were not known until cricket came at the beginning of the eighteenth century. Indoors all sorts of card games were played from whist, which was well established, to cribbage that was new; a great deal of gambling took place among the nobility and better-off gentry; horse racing at Newmarket and elsewhere was extremely popular in the reign of Charles II. Billiards and chess were much played, and backgammon had been introduced. Wagers were staked on nearly all games, including tennis and bowls. Music was reckoned an essential part of every gentleman's education as well as every lady's. Concert-going and theatre-going in London

Tennis

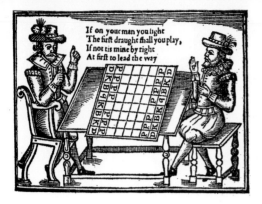

If on your man you light
The first draught shall you play,
If not tis mine by right
At first to lead the way

A game of chess

received an impetus after the middle of the seventeenth century. The Court was a noble patron of masques or amateur theatricals in the first half of the century. Money was spent lavishly on clothes and wigs, which became more and more elaborate after the restoration of Charles II.

THE GENTRY AND POLITICS

Though the average gentleman in Stuart England passed much of his life in hunting and shooting, in eating and drinking, in being hospitable to his neighbours, and helpful or condescending to his inferiors, it must not be thought that he was either stupid or uneducated. Certainly he had a record for extravagance; when Marmaduke Rawdon, a merchant and bachelor, was offered the daughter of another merchant in marriage along with £3,000 in ready money, her father said 'he would rather marry his daughter to a merchant of good fame that knew how to get his living and preserve the portion he gave with his daughter than to a gentleman of good estates that only knew how to spend money'. However, most gentle-

A Court masque

men did pretty well out of their rents and farms or out of their marriages (most merchants did not at all object to their daughters marrying into the landed gentry); they read books and later news-letters or newspapers and kept in touch with what was going on by visits to the county town or to the capital. The expansion of the gentry in the century before the civil wars contributed to a growing sense of their own political

78

importance. In the House of Commons, led by men like John Eliot and John Hampden, wealthy landowners with vigorous ideas about their political grievances, the English squires assembled in parliamentary session asserted themselves even more emphatically than they had done in the Elizabethan parliaments.

Though they were divided in their loyalties during the civil wars, nearly all these upper-class people had their friends or relatives on the other side of the line and do not appear to have suffered material financial losses once it was all over. Naturally some of the smaller gentry went to the wall

Restoration fashion

both before and after, but that was usually owing to their own carelessness or extravagance rather than to the winds of political and economic change. In most parliaments there was an independent group of country gentlemen who could neither be cajoled nor bribed. In vain James II attempted to bring pressure upon them to support the lifting of the restrictions on his fellow Roman Catholics. But the majority remained true to their exclusionist Anglican beliefs: after all, many of the nobility and better-to-do gentry remembered that their own family fortunes had been founded on the destruction of the Roman Catholic Church. Where their treasure was, there were their hearts also. So after all the ups and downs of the Stuart era, in which they watched one monarch lose his head and another his throne, the squire and Anglican parson marched forward together confidently into the warm glow of the eighteenth century.

Further Reading

Andrew Browning (ed.), *Memoirs of Sir John Reresby*, 1936
Elizabeth Burton, *The Jacobeans at Home* (illustrated), 1962

Elizabeth Godfrey, *Home Life under the Stuarts* (illustrated), 1903

Marmaduke Rawdon, *Memoirs* (Camden Society), 1853

I. A. Roots and D. H. Pennington, *The Committee at Stafford, 1643–1645*, 1957

Gladys Scott Thomson, *Life in a Noble Household, 1641–1700* (illustrated), 1936

Lawrence Stone, *The Crisis of the Aristocracy, 1558–1641*, 1965

R. H. Tawney, *The Rise of the Gentry* (*Economic History Review*), 1941

Hugh Trevor-Roper, *The Gentry, 1540–1640*, 1953

V

The Capital and the Court

The increasing predominance of London in the economic life of the kingdom had been generally recognized ever since the Reformation. When James I came to the throne it contained one-twelfth to one-tenth of the entire population; the port handled three-quarters of the nation's foreign trade; and, in one way or another, the capital contributed largely to the revenues of the Crown and nobility; above all, the financial resources of the country were more and more concentrated in the City of London. Individual financiers and bankers made short-term and medium-term loans to the Treasury long before the Bank of England was established.

The Lord Mayor of London and his aldermen

In its broadest sense London comprised more than the City proper, a crowded square mile, flanked by its wall and its gates; it was linked with the City of Westminster, where was situated the palace of Whitehall, which housed the royal Court and much of the machinery of government. Whereas the City proper was governed by a Lord Mayor, 24 aldermen, and a Common Council, all duly elected, Westminster was ruled by a high steward, chosen by the dean and chapter

81

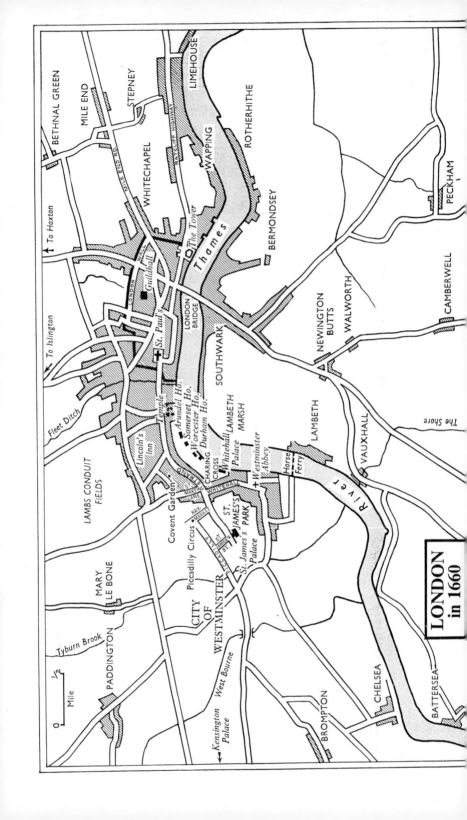

LONDON
in 1660

BETHNAL GREEN
MILE END
STEPNEY
WHITECHAPEL
LIMEHOUSE
WAPPING
RATCLIFF HIGHWAY
MILE END RD.
ROTHERHITHE
PECKHAM

To Hoxton
To Islington
Guildhall
St. Paul's
Temple
The Tower
Thames
LONDON BRIDGE
BERMONDSEY
CAMBERWELL

Fleet Ditch
Lincoln's Inn
Arundel Ho.
Somerset Ho.
Worcester Ho.
Durham Ho.
CHARING CROSS
Whitehall
LAMBETH MARSH
SOUTHWARK
NEWINGTON BUTTS
WALWORTH

LAMBS CONDUIT FIELDS
Covent Garden
THE STRAND
MARTING LANE
WHITEHALL
Westminster Palace
Westminster Abbey
Horse Ferry
LAMBETH
VAUXHALL
The Shore

MARY LE BONE
Piccadilly Circus
PICCADILLY
HAY-MARKET
ST. JAMES'S STREET
ST. JAMES'S PARK
St. James's Palace
CITY OF WESTMINSTER

Tyburn Brook
PADDINGTON
West Bourne
Kensington Palace
BROMPTON
CHELSEA
BATTERSEA
River

½
0   Mile

of Westminster abbey, though 12 burgesses and 12 assistants, who were appointed for life, worked with him. Southwark, lying across the river Thames south of London Bridge, occupied an anomalous position, for though it belonged to the City of London it possessed neither an alderman nor a common councillor.

Even before the Stuart period the monarchy had been much concerned over the growth of London. A proclamation by Queen Elizabeth I forbidding new building within three miles of the city gates referred to the overcrowding of rooms and tenements. Expansion had been going on eastwards towards the villages of Stepney, Limehouse, and Wapping; but in the seventeenth century expansion also began westwards towards the fashionable village of Kensington and even on to the little fishing village of Putney. King James I issued no fewer than nine proclamations attempting to prevent the further growth of London; Charles I also published proclamations forbidding building on new foundations; under Oliver Cromwell a tax was not only imposed upon new buildings, but the money actually collected. The Great Fire in 1666 destroyed 13,000 houses, but this caused merely a temporary check on the rate of expansion. By the reign of Queen Anne London was almost twice as populous as it had been in the reign of Queen Elizabeth I.

Inevitably the City of London had political influence deriving from its financial strength. But up to 1639 its leaders supported the monarchy. In that year when the Crown appealed to the City for men and money to use in what was called the first Bishops' War against the Scots some of the commoners wanted to hand a petition to the King outlining a number of grievances, including the 'multitude of monopolies and patents' at the same time as he was presented with a meagre loan of £5,000. However, that proposal was rejected; it was not until the very eve of the first civil war that the leading Puritans in the City organized a coup d'état in conjunction with the Puritan leaders at Westminster. The City then supported Parliament against the King throughout the civil wars, but afterwards its principal merchants gradually tired of the Cromwellian Protectorate and enthusiastically welcomed back Charles II in 1660. The City

Part of Howland Great Dock, Deptford

also turned against James II, welcomed William and Mary, and gave enthusiastic assistance to Queen Anne during the war against France. But it would be wrong to assume that the political opinions of the City Fathers were those of the country as a whole; indeed the economic and political influence of the capital on the government was widely resented in the provinces.

London was an industrial town and busy seaport as well as the heart of the kingdom's commerce and finance. Moreover it was a cosmopolitan city: Edmund Howes, the continuator of Stow's famous Elizabethan *Surveys* of London, thought that the alien residents and the marriages of citizens to foreigners contributed very largely to the growing prosperity of the capital in the first half of the seventeenth century. In 1635 it contained about 4–5,000 aliens and London's industries included shipbuilding, silk-weaving, paper-making, brewing, brick-making, and cloth manufacture. The seaport contained 20,000 craft in Charles I's reign; a new dock was built at Blackwall in 1614; Stepney and Deptford were said to be 'cradles of the royal navy'; the river was both a port estuary and a public highway. The Thames had 30 landing places, but there was only the one bridge over the river, London Bridge, which was carried on 18 arches, was a famous shopping centre and was always crowded with people and traffic. So up and down the river the ferrymen,

London Bridge, c. 1700

a rough, blasphemous, and frightening crowd, did a roaring trade. The roads through London, their direction largely prescribed by the position of the gates, were cobbled and uneven and mostly narrow; traffic jams were even worse than they became in modern

A ferryman

times. Sir William Davenant, the playwright wrote: 'Sure, your ancestors contrived your narrow streets in the days of street barrows before these great engines, carts, were invented.' And the traffic was worsened by the increasing numbers of hackney coaches in the latter half of the Stuart period. The Thames ferrymen, who numbered 2,000 in 1676, vainly attempted to prevent or restrict the hiring of these carriages in the reign of Charles II, but were unable to do so. Cromwell had used a hackney coach on the last occasion he drove to dissolve parliament; Princess Anne took a hackney coach to escape from Whitehall during the revolution of 1688.

It has sometimes been argued that neither the sanitation in London nor the lighting at night was as bad in the seventeenth century as later generations believed. It is true that in 1662 commissioners for scavenging were appointed in London by an act of parliament and the noisome character of the City was mitigated by the numerous open spaces and by the muck being carried away by the river tides. But the great number of slums, the lack of sanitary

A hackney coach

arrangements in the majority of the houses, the prevalence of poverty, unemployment, and crime, the frequent plagues, the existence of such industries as soap-boiling, the increasing use of coal for burning in domestic chimneys all contributed to the pall of smoke and dust that often hung over the city and the streams of filth that flowed in open sewers through its streets. At night the City was intermittently lit by lanterns and torches and a watch provided. But again the evidence of playwrights and others about the dangers in town

A fire-engine in action

at night, the multitude of thieves and footpads, though they were cruelly punished if caught, and the need for private citizens to hire boys or wenches to light them home is pretty conclusive. King William III, who suffered from asthma, refused to live in London at all, preferring to create a palace at Kensington; Oliver Cromwell spent as much time as he could at Hampton Court; James I only spent a minimum amount or time each year at Whitehall. The villages of Islington, Hackney, Chelsea, Hammersmith, and Hampstead were all pleasant enough to live in. So was the fashionable West End as it extended west and north-west of St James's Square.

In Charles I's reign Haymarket and Piccadilly were still rural, though it was complained that the springs of water that flowed along Piccadilly were polluted by the few houses that had been built there: on the advice of Inigo Jones, the King's Surveyor, their owner was fined £1,000. But the areas of Leicester Fields, Covent Garden, and St Martin's Lane and later St James's Street and Arlington Street became more and more fashionable. The populating of London's West End received a fresh impulse when Queen Anne occupied St James's Palace as her London residence.

Indeed London, to use the term in its broadest sense, exemplified the contrasts in the kingdom as a whole; on the one side were the overcrowded tenements of the City poor, on the other, the magnificent houses of the nobility that lined the Strand. For example, the north wing of Bedford House held a long terrace room, hung with magnificent tapestries and furnished with chairs and stools covered with red and green velvet and silk. Such a house had gardens and ample stables and stairs that led down to the river. Besides the palaces of the nobility the capital contained at the outset of the Stuart period

The Strand from the river, with Arundel House in the foreground

The City skyline before the Great Fire, from

125 churches including Westminster Abbey and St Paul's cathedral. The spire of St Paul's had fallen, the nave had decayed, and the interior was as much used as a place for gossip, chaffering, and games as for services, but it still ennobled London's skyline as seen across the river. The Tower of London was another impressive building, which was employed alike as a state prison, an arsenal, a mint, and a zoo. On the south bank of the Thames or Bankside was a theatre much frequented by fledgling lawyers from the Temple and other London Inns. Many of the two-storeyed houses in the City were built of wood, to which fires were a perpetual threat. The Great Fire of London destroyed, in addition to houses, 84 churches, St Paul's cathedral, and the Guildhall. But Westminster Abbey, the Tower, Lincoln's Inn and Covent Garden all escaped. The people of London took the conflagration calmly. 'It is not to be expressed', said James Yonge, the Plymouth surgeon afterwards, 'how dismal it looked nor how unconcerned most people that passed were at it. . . .' Only Samuel Pepys and a few others displayed disinterested energy in trying to put out the fires.

In fact the fire afforded a stimulus to building. Brick houses replaced wooden ones; open spaces, in private hands, were built over to recoup losses; gradually the palatial houses on the Strand disappeared, while the area to the north was profitably developed. The Earl of Bedford, who was lucky enough to own the Covent Garden area, made a great deal of money out of it:

the Swan Theatre to the Tower of London

St Paul's church and the piazza there were admired by foreign visitors. Much of the Strand was used for trading; Covent Garden market had been established before the fire; and various exchanges to house dress shops and the like were built. One exchange, which earned the nickname of 'the whores' nest', however, was a failure, since few people took shops in it.

The Great Fire stimulated the migration of fashionable London society towards the West End, whose real birth belongs to the reign of Charles II. St James's Square, where it was customary to find homes for royal mistresses, long remained very open and was used occasionally for firework displays: but it also became a rubbish tip, filled with dead cats and dogs. In general the West End was becoming a dignified residential area, the resorts of beaux and belles who patronized the new

Covent Garden: the piazza and St Paul's Church, by Inigo Jones

Patrons of the new coffee houses

coffee houses. And although the chance was not taken for a complete replanning of the City, as advocated by Sir Christopher Wren, the Fire was followed by the building of the new St Paul's cathedral, many of Wren's city churches, some wider streets, spacious squares, a beautified Covent Garden, and the development of Pall Mall and Piccadilly.

Yet the attractions of the West End and the pleasures of watching high society driving through Hyde Park in their coaches still contrasted with the squalidness of the City's underworld, the city of Ned Ward's *London Spy*, with its dark houses, smutty prints, and blind beggars. Like all big ports, London was a wicked city, no place for the innocent. A gang of thieves and outlaws, who previously concentrated in a district known as Alsatia, were later organized by Jonathan Wild, a Jekyll-Hyde character, both a receiver of stolen goods and an active magistrate. After the Restoration the brutality, poverty, and ignorance rampant in London's East End slums did not lie far from the fashionable and cultured world of Westminster. Perpetual warfare was waged between the respectable and religious, on one side, and the cruel and criminal, on the other. It was then said that 'the miles between Hell and any place on earth' were 'shorter than those between London and St Albans'.

90

THE PALACE OF WHITEHALL

The City of London was joined to Westminster by the village of Charing Cross. Westminster contained the parliament house, the Abbey, and the vast rambling 'rabbit warren' or 'rookery' of a Palace. Although the monarchy possessed several other great houses, Whitehall remained the office buildings of the executive and the principal residence of the monarch until the end of the seventeenth century. Inigo Jones built a palace at Greenwich for James I's Queen; Christopher Wren converted Kensington House into a palace for the benefit of William III; and St James's Palace, originally built for Henry VIII on the site of a former leper hospital, was lived in by Queen Anne. But Whitehall was long the recognized centre of national administration, the place where foreign diplomatists and visitors were interviewed and entertained, the heart of London society, the fountain of honours, privileges, and rewards. In its buildings, which were of all shapes and sizes, there dwelt besides the King hundreds of his officers and servants. Covering an area of 23 acres and containing 2,000 rooms, it could be approached either from the river at Whitehall steps or by a narrow lane with King Street gate at one end and the Holbein gate at the other. Charles I, a man of taste, would have liked to knock the whole place down and have it rebuilt by his distinguished Surveyor

Whitehall Palace, showing the banqueting house by Inigo Jones

General, Inigo Jones. But Inigo Jones, who was full of ideas, and would have been pleased not only to rebuild the Palace but much of the capital as well, was only allowed, after the former banqueting house had been burnt down in 1619, to construct a new one, which had its ceilings painted by Rubens and has remained intact until the present day.

Parts of the Palace were virtually open to the public, if they could get past the porter at the Court gate. The Great Court, for example, the Terrace, the Stone Gallery, which contained many lovely paintings, and the Outer Chamber were all habitually thronged by various classes of visitors or suitors for royal or official favours. From the Great Chamber of Whitehall Palace a distinguished visitor would be conducted through the King's Presence Chamber, open to all who were entitled to appear at Court, to the Privy Chamber, closed except to a privileged few. The courtiers had access both to the Presence Chamber and the Privy Gardens and could enjoy such sports as took place in the Cockpit, Tiltyard, and chief tennis court on the other side of the lane. But the King did most of his business in his Bedchamber or Council Room, while other sets of apartments were assigned to the Queen and princes or princesses,

Charles I dining in public

each of whom held their own courts. The King dined in public about midday where he might be gazed at in all his glory from the galleries around the banqueting hall, but he supped in private, as did the courtiers in their own quarters. In James I's time 'at nine o'clock began the elaborate procedure known as the "Order of All Night" with the King going to bed, the doors of the Privy Chamber being locked, the guard being mounted in the Great Chamber, and the password being given for the night' (Akrigg).

The principal officers of the royal household were the Lord Chamberlain, who had a staff of 750 under him, not all on full-time, the Lord Steward, who was responsible for the household needs of the palace, and the Master of the Horse, who looked after the outdoor staff. Another high post at court was that of Earl Marshal, who was expected to be present on all state occasions and was traditionally the Duke of Norfolk. But none of these royal officers did much of the work themselves: James I's Master of the Horse was his favourite, Buckingham. Another favourite, Somerset, had been Lord Chamberlain. These were in fact largely honorific offices which brought their holders into daily contact with the monarch and enabled them to exert patronage and pocket large sums of money.

Apart from the three chief posts at Court, other principal royal officers were the Lord Chancellor (or Keeper), the Lord Treasurer, the Lord Privy Seal, the Lord President of the Council, the Lord High Constable, and the Lord High Admiral. But there were other valuable offices at Court, such as the Comptroller and Master of the Household and political posts such as the Secretaryship of State. And of course the archbishops and bishops were personally appointed by the Crown. But no precise distinction could be drawn during the Stuart period between ornamental Court functionaries and hard-working officers of state. John Chamberlain remarked that 'the court of the king of England is a monarchy within a monarchy, consisting of ecclesiastical, civil and military persons and government'.

King James I spent only about a third of each year in White-hall Palace. Though usually there at Christmas, Easter, and in the late autumn, he liked to occupy as much time as he possibly

James I hawking

could in the hunting field, either in his own country estates or those of his richest subjects whom he favoured, as for example Sir Oliver Cromwell's house of Hinchingbrooke at Huntingdon. His favourite hunting lodges were at Royston and Newmarket in Cambridgeshire where he spent much of the summer, although he usually enjoyed a few weeks at Hampton Court and Windsor Castle. When the King was known to be at Whitehall country gentry would come flocking up to London in search of favours. But Whitehall was an uncomfortable place to live in and by the reign of Charles II the King's mistresses and courtiers were moving into the West End. In 1663 Lord St Albans explained in a petition to the King that: 'the beauty of this great town and the convenience of the Court are defective in point of houses fit for the dwellings of noblemen and other persons of quality'; and therefore asked permission to build in the area of St James's. In the early part of the century a fair was held each spring in the neighbourhood of St James's Palace, but after 1636 it was moved north and gave its name to modern Mayfair.

THE EARLY STUART COURTS

While the King's Court might be considered a large and rather complicated administrative machine, like the 'Whitehall' of the present century, with hundreds of officials and clerks, comprising not merely the lush fountain of concessions and offices, the hub of the diplomatic service, and even the high courts of law, it also set a pattern for the social life of the country. 'Looking back at the Jacobean court,' writes Professor Akrigg, 'the modern observer must be impressed by its extravagant luxury, its unruliness, its sycophancy, and its all-pervasive graft and corruption.' When James I arrived from Scotland with his wife and children he felt sure that he had inherited a gold mine. He was accompanied by a host of hungry Scotsmen, and the Englishmen he favoured, the Cecils and the Howards, were by no means behind them in their avaricious tapping of his inordinate bounty. The expenses of his household were soon twice those of Queen Elizabeth's and the royal debt steadily mounted. Spasmodic efforts were made to economize, and for a time the genius of Lionel Cranfield put matters right. But nothing could check the royal prodigality for long. The King could not deny a kindness to one he liked or be mean to those in distress, unless they annoyed him. He distributed and sold titles: baronetcies, created by him, at first fetched £1,000 each; he farmed taxes, auctioned patents, and permitted monopolies that raised the price of necessities as well as luxuries; in spite of promises from Queen Elizabeth a great many things, from starch to playing cards, were subjected to licences in the hands of courtiers.

The court was notoriously corrupt. King James knew it, but was cynical. He told the Venetian ambassador once that if he were to execute everyone who defrauded the state, as was the practice in Venice, he would have no subjects left. Although the King himself laid down high moral principles in his writings and speeches, the immorality of the Court was known everywhere. In a contemporary ballad a contrast was drawn between the old courtiers of Queen Elizabeth I's reign and the new flourishing gallants:

Who kept a brace of painted creatures to be at his hand
And be drunk in a new tavern till he be not able to stand.

Lady Anne Clifford, herself something of a Puritan, remarked on how at the beginning of the reign 'there was much talk . . . how all the ladies about the court had gotten such ill names that it was grown a scandalous place'. There may have been some exaggeration about the extent of the licentiousness and drunkenness that prevailed; but the King behaved himself in public like a homosexual, fawning on his favourites, Somerset, Buckingham, and the rest, and being separated from his wife before her early death.

James's son, Charles I, who preferred his father's precepts to his behaviour, promptly put an end to all that. The boorish and unruly courtiers were quickly warned. 'On his accession,' observes Dr Wedgwood, 'the broad Scots jokes and drunken romps which had amused his father soon ceased.' The Court became formal and dignified: no one was allowed to sit in the royal presence. But Charles was as extravagant as his predecessor: whereas James had been fond of hunting and theology, his son became the patron of arts and literature. The King and Queen themselves regularly performed elaborate masques written for them by the poets and musicians of the time. As late as 1640 Charles I appeared in a masque by Sir William Davenant, the poet laureate. The King also collected Italian paintings and brought over artists from abroad to work for him in Whitehall. After the death of the Duke of Buckingham in 1628, the King became devoted to his young French wife, Queen Henrietta Maria, and indulged her frivolities, such as her passion for dancing. The courtiers soon took the hint offered by the King's example. There was less licentiousness and the nobility even made a display of being faithful to their wives. Admirably, some of them also imitated the King in their patronage of the arts: for example, the Earl of Arundel brought over the distinguished Bohemian artist and engraver, Wenceslaus Hollar to England in 1637. To Hollar we owe many of the views of London and Windsor that give us so much visual insight into the life of the Stuart age.

Windsor Castle: a view by Wenceslaus Hollar, 1644

Perhaps the very happiness and self-sufficiency of King Charles I and his wife in their formal and beautiful Court had its evil consequences. They lived in a world they had fashioned for themselves: the monarch did not have the very human defects of his conceited, intelligent, and irascible father. Their children tended to be left to their own devices and when the storm of civil war broke, when Charles I was defeated and his wife forced into exile, the two princes, who were to become the next English monarchs, wandered over the face of the earth without any principle to guide them other than the urge to regain their lost inheritance. Thus when Charles II was restored to the throne in 1660 he brought back with him not the restrained dignity of his father's Court but the careless licentiousness of his grandfather's.

There was in any case an understandable reaction against the seriousness of the Court of Oliver Cromwell. Cromwell himself did not care much for Whitehall and spent his week-ends at Hampton Court. Nor was his Court exceptionally austere. Like the Stuarts, he enjoyed hunting and hawking. He was the patron of good music; he appreciated his glass of ale or wine and a pipe of tobacco. He preserved some of Charles I's paintings at Hampton Court and patronized artists like Samuel Cooper, a great English painter. But he did not think much of foreign 'kickshaws' and his wife never entirely adjusted herself to her high position or forgot that she had once been the busy wife of a small farmer.

THE LATER STUART COURTS

By contrast Charles II's Court naturally seemed extremely lax, even if perhaps an exaggerated idea is obtained from the scandalous sources of the reign, such as Samuel Pepys's diary—for Pepys got most of his information at second-hand—or the memoirs of the Count of Gramont, which are unreliable. Nevertheless the stories of Court life in those days are stranger than any fiction: how a baby was born on a ballroom floor, how Charles II forgave Colonel Thomas Blood who kidnapped the Duke of Ormonde and stole the Crown jewels from the Tower;

Charles II dancing at a ball with his sister Mary, Princess of Orange

how the French King sent over a young Breton girl to become
his brother monarch's mistress (she became the Duchess of
Portsmouth in due course); how Charles II, having exposed
the lies of the perjured informer, Titus Oates, allowed him to
send many innocent men to their deaths; how the second Duke
of Buckingham killed the husband of his mistress, the Countess
of Shrewsbury, in a duel and went unpunished. Although
duelling was supposed to be illegal, it frequently took place
and was condoned by the Court.

Originally the King was surrounded by men whom he had
inherited as loyal servants from his father or who had assisted
in his restoration, Clarendon, Southampton, Ormonde, Nicholas,
Monk, and Morice; but gradually they were replaced by less
scrupulous politicians who knew how to pander to the King's
whims and obtain the support of the 'buffoons and ladies of
pleasure', as John Evelyn called them, about the Court. Then
again there was a reaction when Danby tried to rally Parliament
and Church behind the King, though he lacked the King's real
confidence: men like Nottingham, Guildford, Leoline Jenkins,
and Halifax were all of high calibre and integrity. Thus it would
be wrong to decry the quality of all the men and women who
served Charles II. Nonetheless, the King himself set a poor
example by his extreme Francophilism, his laziness, and his
obsession with the other sex. Sir John Reresby tried to excuse
him at the beginning of his reign when he wrote that:

The King, as he was of an age and vigour for it followed his pleasures. And if amongst these love prevailed with him more than others, he was thus far excusable, besides that his pleasure led to it, women seemed to be the aggressors, and I have since heard the King say did sometimes offer themselves to his embraces. The two dukes (James and Henry) were no less lovers of the sex than himself.

But when six or seven years passed and the King got rid of his old councillors and allowed himself to be influenced by his principal mistresses, even the most enthusiastic royalists began to despair. John Evelyn wrote in 1666 apropos a general fast ordered after the great plague, the Dutch war, and the fire of London:

> The most dismal judgments could be inflicted and indeed but what we highly deserved for our prodigious ingratitude, burning lusts, dissolute court, profane and abominable lives, under such dispensations of God's continued favour in restoring Church, Prince, and people from our late intestine calamities, of which we were altogether unmindful, even to astonishment.

James II at once set about reforming the Court when he came to the throne in 1685. He did not approve of the easygoing manners, morals, or policies that prevailed under Charles II. The French ambassador reported that it was the new King's intention 'to observe every formality and to preserve exactly all the externals of royal dignity'. Duelling, swearing, and drunkenness became taboo; the King gave particular instructions that no courtier was to be drunk in the presence of the Queen. James II also had no public mistress, although Catherine Sedley who had long been his mistress, would have liked to move into the apartments of the Duchess of Portsmouth. Instead, however, she was provided with a house in St James's Square.

In general James II's Court was better behaved, more decorous, and less extravagant than that of his brother. The Queen, Mary of Modena, was upset over Catherine Sedley, but continued her efforts to produce an heir. When she looked pale, one of her confessors objected to her using rouge. She was cheered, however, by having her own apartments in Whitehall reconstructed and redecorated under the supervision of Christopher Wren, with Verrio painting the ceilings and Grinling Gibbons carving the overmantel in her bedchamber. The King also lent his patronage to the French academic painter, Nicolas Largillière.

James had his faults, but the atmosphere at his Court was by no means philistine. With the arrival of William III in London all this changed again. Even William's admirer, Lord Macaulay, wrote that 'he seldom came forth from his closet; and when he appeared in the public rooms, he stood among the crowd of courtiers and ladies, stern and abstracted, making no jest and smiling to none'. His wife, Queen Mary II, was affable but a little austere; she discouraged scandal-mongers and any kind of vicious habits at the Court. But William could not stand Westminster air or the fogs and smoke of winter and removed himself first to Hampton Court and then to Kensington House, which he bought from the Earl of Nottingham. Hampton Court

Hampton Court: the south front (right), designed by Wren, was built 1689-1701

was improved by the same artists employed by James II—Wren, Verrio, and Gibbons. There was no longer a Court or any social gathering in the rabbit warren of Whitehall and in 1698 the entire palace was burnt down except for the banqueting house of Inigo Jones. During the first years of the reign of William and Mary the King was abroad much of the year while the Queen presided over both the Court and the administration. After her death in 1694, the coldness with which William treated the English nobility, many of whom he, justifiably, did not trust, and his propensity for Dutch favourites further damaged Court life; and before the King's death in 1702 the English upper classes were flocking round his successor, Queen Anne.

Anne, like her sister, was charitable and highly moral and had a sense of her own dignity. One of her first proclamations was aimed at the punishment of immorality and vice and the promotion of piety and virtue. The debauchery practised at the Court of Charles II was now a thing of the past. Few shadows fell on the Queen's Ministers or their wives. But drunkenness, gambling, and duelling were quite common in Queen Anne's London; the monarch herself was a passionate enthusiast for card-playing and enjoyed a tipple. Anne moved back from Kensington Palace to St James's Palace, but she kept Court there as little as possible. She spent much of her time at Windsor Castle or taking the waters in Bath. At St James's she entertained only her Ministers and her women favourites and their friends, and she was a model wife. Gilbert Burnet, Bishop of Salisbury, wrote of her:

> Queen Anne is easy of access and hears everything gently, but she opens herself to so few, and is so cold and general in her answers, that people soon find that the chief application is to be made to her ministers and favourites . . . she had laid down the splendour of a court too much, and eats privately; so that except on Sundays, and a few hours twice or thrice a week at night in the drawing room, she appears so little that her court, as it were, is abandoned.

Thus at the close of the Stuart age the royal Court had virtually ceased to be the centre of London society. The capital had by now virtually doubled its size and population, while

Queen Anne presiding over a Cabinet meeting

parliament was taking an increasingly important part in the affairs of the kingdom. Indeed Queen Anne was the last monarch to preside regularly over Cabinet meetings; and in the next reign Sir Robert Walpole was to become the first clearly acknowledged Prime Minister of England.

Further Reading

G. P. V. Akrigg, *Jacobean Pageant* (illustrated), 1962
N. G. Brett-James, *The Growth of Stuart London* (illustrated), 1953
J. P. Kenyon, *The Stuarts* (illustrated), 1958
David Ogg, *England in the Reign of Charles II*, 1955
— —, *England in the Reigns of James II and William III*, 1955
Valerie Pearl, *London and the Outbreak of the Puritan Revolution*, 1961
G. M. Trevelyan, *England Under Queen Anne*, 1930–4

VI

Church and State

'God will comfort and supply the wants of his poor servants', wrote the Lancashire apprentice, Roger Lowe, in 1663. Throughout the Stuart age the mass of the English people, to whichever class they belonged and whatever sort of Christian teaching they accepted, believed fervently in the ever-present reality of God in their lives. The huge uncertainties of dwellers upon earth, the epidemics, the floods or fires, the weather that froze the seeds or ruined the harvests, the constant poverty and unemployment, above all the perpetual reminders of mortality in the frequency of death among young children and their mothers made men and women cling to their faith lest they had nothing else to cling to. If things went well for them, they expressed their gratitude to the Almighty: for example the Reverend Ralph Josselin wrote in a time of plague of 'God's good providences' in preserving his and his family's health and allowing him to sell a bag of hops at a profit.

But if things went badly, then God also had a purpose. Sir John Eliot wrote as he approached his death in prison: 'Oh, the infinite mercy of our Master . . . how it abounds to us that are unworthy of His service.' Oliver Cromwell spoke of 'the happiness we all pant after and live for', when he wrote to console a brother officer for the death of his son in battle. Nicholas Culpepper likewise reminded himself: 'If I do die, I do but go out of a miserable world to receive a crown of immortality.' But suppose one was snatched from the brink, then the Lord had also shown his goodness. 'I received on myself the sentence of death', Cromwell once wrote to General

Fairfax, 'that I might learn to trust to Him that raiseth from the dead.' If one but realized how little the world was worth, surely it was 'a blessed thing to die daily'.

The Christian had to trust that God knew his business. 'I had a very sickly day,' wrote Lowe once, 'but the Lord instigated the pain.' Lowe knew that if he believed and prayed, God would display his mercy. 'I was somewhat pensive all day in consideration of my unsettlements in this world, but yet most comforted in trusting God'; and again 'God will arise and show pity on his distressed servant'. The vast majority of English Christians were predestinarians when King James I came to the throne: that is to say they believed, as John Calvin had taught, that each and all of them were destined for the Life Everlasting, but the other fellows—the sinners—could not be saved. Men then thought that it was logical for an all-powerful Creator, who had planned events, to choose those who were to be saved or to be damned. James I himself was a Calvinist; his second archbishop of Canterbury was a Calvinist; so were many bishops; so were the King's representatives at the Synod of Dort which was held in Holland in 1618 to discuss predestina-

Preaching at St Paul's Cross, in the presence of James I

tion and which upheld the Calvinist position. It was not doctrinal differences that divided the Church of England at the outset of the Stuart period, but questions of organization and ritual.

Mrs John Hutchinson, a Puritan, wrote in her life of her husband: 'Upon the great revolution which took place at the accession of Queen Elizabeth to the Crown, the nation became divided into three great factions, the Papist, the State-protestant, and the more religious zealots who afterwards were branded with the name of Puritan.' Before the accession of Elizabeth England had been a Roman Catholic country under her sister, Mary I. Slowly Elizabeth had restored the Church of her father, who had repudiated the Pope and hammered the monks. But she had to contend, on the one side, against the old 'papists' and, on the other, against the new extreme Protestants or Puritans. After James I succeeded Elizabeth he hoped to conciliate the English Roman Catholics and meet some at least of the demands of the Puritans. He failed to do either; the Catholics were concerned in conspiracies against him; a number of Puritan clergy gave up their livings rather than conform with existing practices. When Charles I came to the throne, he, an Anglican-bred monarch, never forgetful throughout his life of his religious upbringing, even during many months of temptation in Spain, found himself the head of 'a young and insecure church . . . feebly rooted in the affections of the people' (Wedgwood). Indeed the Church of England or 'State-protestant' was still formulating and fortifying its intellectual position. Its protagonists embraced the defence of the spiritual golden mean invented by Richard Hooker; and in men like William Chillingworth, John Donne, Nicholas Ferrar, George Herbert, Godfrey Goodman, John Hales, and Jeremy Taylor commanded a number of distinguished and gifted advocates. But at first their arguments did not penetrate widely or deeply. The parish clergy as a whole varied in their quality, their characters, and their status. They read morning and evening prayers from the naves of their churches; they expected their congregations to attend communion services three times a year; some of them delivered set homilies about the moral duties of husband, wife, parents, and subjects. But many of them were too busy trying to

105

supplement their miserable stipends to make much of an impression. And so the serious-minded members of their congregations were open to attack from fanatical Protestant reformers or devoted Roman Catholic missionaries.

It must be remembered that the Church and State were essentially one. It was generally accepted by the ruling class, whatever their precise religious professions were, that religion was needed to sustain obedience to those in authority, whether they were kings or ministers, husbands or fathers, employers or justices, overseers of the poor or village constables. Every

Popular piety

member of the commonwealth, wrote Richard Hooker, is also a member of the Church of England. King Charles I—like his son, James II later—recognized the power that could be wielded from the pulpits. The parish was a unit both of the Church and of the State. The churchwardens were responsible both for the upkeep of the fabric of the church and also for the relief of the poor. In one Midland village churchwardens not only organized the purchase of bread and wine for the communion services, but also paid for moles, hedgehogs, and other vermin that were caught and cleared from the village fields. At least until the middle of the seventeenth century the justices of the peace and the church courts shared between them the handling of the social and moral problems of the rural community. And if the State was unified, so must the Church be also.

After the restoration of Charles II a golden age dawned for the Church of England. More money became available, at any rate for the bishops and deans. The ritualists had their hour of triumph and then gave way to the cooler air of a broader, 'rationalist' faith. For a time the government stood four-square behind the religious monopoly of the Church of England. Yet it never recovered completely from the blows that had rained upon it during the Puritan revolution which sent Charles I as an Anglican martyr to his doom; by giving the dissenters their heads for nearly 20 years it ensured that nonconformity would survive, even if it were temporarily driven down. In 1689 the toleration of nonconformist worship was conceded by the government of William and Mary and religious dissent became a permanent factor in the English way of life. From then on Church and State ceased to be identical, even though the non-conformists and the Roman Catholics continued for another century and a half to be excluded from the full privileges of citizenship.

PURITANISM

Puritanism began as a movement inside the Church of England that aimed at the destruction of the remnants of Roman Catholic ritual from which its adherents wanted the English Church to be purified. It rejected the sacramental aspect of Christianity, questioned the right of bishops to exert secular powers, and stressed the importance of the interpretation of the bible by individual believers. While the Puritan felt certain that the true Christian was justified only by his faith, he thought that his election by God to Salvation bore fruit in his own good works and in his own austere life: indeed these proved both to himself and to others that his Salvation had been attained.

Puritanism took many forms and did not appeal to any one class in the community. The last jailer to whom Queen Elizabeth I entrusted the custody of Mary, Queen of Scots was a Puritan; so later was an archbishop, a few peers, many wealthy gentry, and successful merchants. Above all, it attracted many of the rising middle classes including industrialists and yeomen. Its eloquent preachers in the reign of Queen Elizabeth I and the first two Stuart monarchs also aimed at converting the lower classes. Some Puritans wanted to abolish the bishops altogether and substitute for them a presbyterian system of church government as advocated by John Calvin; some wished entirely to separate themselves from the Church; others, known as Independents, wanted a decentralized Church with real power in the hands of the individual congregations; the Baptists or Anabaptists laid emphasis on the value of the total immersion in water of the convert; the Quakers, the most logical and individualist of all the Puritan sects—who rejected the taking of oaths or the wearing of hats to acknowledge men's authority— were prepared to put their trust in the spirit of God manifesting itself during their meetings.

In the course of the reign of Charles I the revivalist movement represented by the Puritans gathered strength. A counterattack was launched by William Laud, who was appointed Archbishop of Canterbury in 1633: a keen ritualist, he came to doubt the doctrine of the predestination of the individual Christian to salvation, in which most Anglicans and nearly all Puritans believed and continued to believe until the eighteenth century and beyond. But the Puritans had many supporters in high places; indeed the bulk of the members of the parliaments that met in 1640 were Puritan in sympathy. So although Laud and his friends managed to suppress certain efforts of Puritan enthusiasts (such as the establishment of lectureships and the buying up of benefices so as to install their own kind of clergy), he did not succeed in checking the movement as his successful Elizabeth predecessor, Whitgift had done. For

Puritan satire on Archbishop Laud

Cavaliers and Roundheads

instance, when Dr John Moseley, the Vicar of Newark, was presented by his own church-wardens for having the communion table moved from where it had been placed as an altar in his church to being used as a table facing east and west, the case was stopped even before it got to court. When a preacher at Ipswich admitted that he could not tell 'whether such was prayer at all that [was] never prayed but out of a book, that a parrot might be taught forms, and an ape imitate gestures', he was removed from his ministry and sent to prison, but ultimately released in 1639 for reasons of health. Many churchwardens at that time refused to inform against their own ministers or fellow parishioners. And by 1642 so rapidly had the Puritan movement progressed that Charles I himself was ready at least to exclude the bishops from the House of Lords. After his defeat in the first civil war he was willing to acquiesce in the imposition of a presbyterian system of church government for three years. Later, his son also committed himself to accepting presbyterianism in England.

But meanwhile the Independent movement had grown apace. So when Oliver Cromwell, himself an Independent, became Lord Protector in 1653 the parish churches were divided up among Presbyterians, Independents and others, while the Quakers, Fifth Monarchists and other extreme sects were left unmolested, though sometimes they tried to break up services. This legalized spiritual anarchy was brought to a prompt end at the restoration.

Ordinary members of the rural congregations came in the course of the years to be accustomed to changes, and many clergy, like the imaginary Vicar of Bray, celebrated in song, adapted themselves to the prevailing fashions. Those who felt most deeply continued to support their own particular faith.

During the Cromwellian period royalists, like John Evelyn, were able to attend Anglican services held in private houses in London. After Charles II came back in 1660 and the Common Prayer Book of 1662 was enforced by law and all sorts of stringent prohibitions imposed on those who refused to conform or to attend the services as laid down in that prayer book, nonconformist ministers were still able to preside over secret gatherings in many parts of the country, often with the acquiescence of the local magistrates. Although for a time there was persecution it was maintained partly because the authorities were genuinely afraid that the nonconformists were plotting against the state. A Quaker, Francis Howgill, was told by a judge in 1663:

> The times being dangerous and things having now a worse appearance than at the last assizes, and people, under the pretence of conscience, violating the laws and hatching treasons and rebellions, although I have nothing of that kind to charge against you, yet seeing you did refuse to take the oath of allegiance at the last assize, the law doth presume such persons to be enemies of the King and Government.

A Quakers' meeting

The 'great persecution' of Charles II's reign left its permanent mark on English nonconformity. It has been reckoned that only about a tenth of the population then still remained loyal to their varying forms of Christian dissent, of whom 40,000 were Quakers. But the movement for toleration now gained momentum. By the reign of James II the persecution had virtually ceased and after 1689 nonconformists were permitted to meet under licence, though they were excluded from public office. In the reign of Queen Anne it was said that there were no fewer than 100,000 nonconformists in London alone attending 88 chapels and that nonconformity was strong in most other towns. Indeed by then nonconformity was acquiring a political and social influence, and some of its adherents even served in parliament or obtained offices by taking communion once a year according to Anglican rites, that is to say 'occasionally conforming'.

ROMAN CATHOLICS

While the Puritans were a developing force in English life, the old religion of Roman Catholicism never wilted in spite of the fiercest persecutions. Acts passed under Elizabeth I

A nonconformist minister

had imposed a crippling fine of £20 a month on Roman Catholics who refused to go to church services on Sundays or Holy Days—these were known as 'recusants', while Catholic priests were liable to death for high treason. Some Catholics fled the country for a time; others went to colleges at Douai and elsewhere to be trained as missionaries to their homeland; and when King James I came to the throne there were already 500 priests secretly at work in England. At first James was lenient towards English Catholics: in May, 1603 he suspended recusancy fines for a year and a half. The Gunpowder Plot organized by extreme Catholics against King and Parliament in 1605, however, resulted in a fresh batch of penalties that were aimed even to catch Catholics who attended church services to avert fines and were known as 'church papists'. Recusants were forbidden to move more than five miles from their homes, to live in London, even to attend Oxford and Cambridge.

Twenty years later the laws against Roman Catholics were relaxed when the negotiations for a French marriage for King Charles I were opened; indeed a secret clause in the marriage treaty guaranteed them freedom of worship. But violent

The Anabaptist.   The Brownist.

all Independants

The Familist.   The Papist.

Sectarianism

anti-papal sentiments were expressed in parliament, making the English Catholics suspicious. 'Fear and tremor have enveloped us,' wrote one of them, 'especially since this treaty with France, that many are afraid to write what otherwise should seem expedient.' Charles I, having married the French Catholic princess and having revealed some pro-Catholic sympathies, was strongly pressed by all his parliaments to revive and enforce the laws against papists. For English Catholics remained pretty numerous, though how numerous is hard to estimate because only figures of actual 'recusants' and not of 'church papists' or others are available. But their numbers seem actually to have increased during the first half of the Stuart period; the Pope thought it worth while to appoint a Vicar Apostolic for England, who was called the Bishop of Chalcedon and had under him archdeacons, vicars, and registrars. The Bishop hid in the houses of Catholic gentry from which he directed his operations, though he met much opposition from Jesuits who refused to recognize his authority. Priests flitted in and out of the country, concealing themselves in the homes of lay sympathizers, for many Englishmen remained loyal to the old religion. In most counties sufficient priests or missionaries were available to supply the spiritual needs of sincere Catholics. How far they were able to practise their religion in peace was determined by the attitude of the constable and other local officers on whom, as usual, the effective administration of the law depended. But a drive was made by the government during Charles I's 'personal rule' to raise money for the Crown by permitting recusants to compound for their fines levied for not attending church; for example, Francis Mathews of Dorset was allowed to do so in 1638 for the modest sum of £12 a year. But in few counties were the penal laws rigorously enforced.

Many Roman Catholics fought for Charles I during the civil wars, notably in the north of England. While the Parliamentarian leaders were violently anti-Catholic, Oliver Cromwell himself when he became Protector was fairly tolerant. For two years he allowed an eccentric Catholic, Sir Kenelm Digby, to stay about his Court putting the case for their lenient treatment. 'In 1654', writes his biographer, 'the Catholics were not badly off, relatively speaking . . . no new recusancy laws were passed and the old ones not much pressed.' Catholics were allowed to attend masses in private and Cromwell assured the French Cardinal Mazarin that they were better off than they had been under Parliament.

At the restoration of Charles II the Catholics hoped for royal gratitude for their loyalty to him, but they were soon disappointed and subjected to the same penal laws that were imposed on the nonconformists. There were still some 500 secular priests and 300–400 Jesuits and others at work in England at this time, while Roman Catholic writers have asserted that one-tenth of the population—that is to say, as

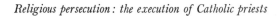

Religious persecution: the execution of Catholic priests

high a proportion of Englishmen as the nonconformists—were Catholics. Just as the Gunpowder Plot had brought persecution and death to English Roman Catholics under James I, so the punishments inflicted after the exposure of the so-called Popish Plot of 1678 injured harmless English Catholics under Charles II. But they survived the years of persecution and in 1685, James II, himself a Roman Catholic, became King of England.

Ever since the Stuarts came to the throne of England Catholicism had been quite strong among the nobility and gentry, while conversions had been effected at the courts of Charles I, Charles II, and James II. Though the Test Acts of Charles II's reign excluded them from public office and from parliament, the penal laws of Elizabeth and her successors that remained on the statute book were by the end of the seventeenth century 'either applied with lenience or not at all'. And even during the long wars against France Roman Catholic services were held in private unmolested. Roman Catholic nobility and gentry often had their private priests and were left alone by their neighbours: the Duke of Devonshire asserted in the reign of Queen Anne that 'he remembered his master, King William saying that he came over to defend the Protestants and not to persecute the Papists'. Thus at the end of 100 years of Stuart rule, despite the reaction against the dissenters after the civil wars and despite the anti-papist frenzy in Charles II's reign, the Church of England was obliged to accept the practising of other forms of the Christian religion than its own by maybe one-fifth of the kingdom, and the English people were being slowly but effectively schooled in notions of liberty of conscience and liberty of worship.

THE MONARCH AND HIS SUBJECTS

Throughout the Stuart period there was an intimate connection between the Church and the State. At the foot of the administrative ladder the churchwardens were, as we have seen, responsible both for much of the social as well as the spiritual welfare of the parish; at the top the monarch was not merely the secular ruler of the kingdom but also the Supreme Governor

of the Church. The Church he governed through his archbishops, bishops, and two convocations of clergy. As head of
the state he was supreme when he sat as king in parliament. So
the King possessed very real powers, and his authority was
enhanced by the fact that he was the Lord's Anointed. The first
Stuart ruler, King James I, is often thought of as having
invented the 'Divine Right of Kings'; but, in fact, all English
monarchs and indeed others in positions of authority right down
to heads of families had long claimed to govern by divine right.

The Lower House of Convocation

Both the Old and the New Testaments had shown that a man
must govern his wife and family; it was on this basis that Sir
Robert Filmer, the favourite political philosopher of the
Royalists, argued persuasively that a paternal monarchy was
prescribed and approved by the Almighty. The ceremony of
the coronation was sacred and significant; and all the Stuart
monarchs exercised the power to lay their hands on their
subjects to cure them of the scrofula or King's Evil.

Even after two political revolutions had taken place the
strength of the Stuart monarchy remained very considerable.

King William III was no constitutional monarch; he selected his own ministers, directed his own foreign policy, and dissolved parliaments when he wished. Indeed a recent historian has claimed that even after the passage of the Bill of Rights 'William III had as high a view of his prerogatives as the [other] Stuarts and intended to rule like Charles II'. Queen Anne could and did dismiss her Ministers as she felt inclined and dissolved parliaments of which she did not approve. The first three Stuarts treated the judges as their officials and advisers not, as Sir Edward Coke had wished, as the arbiters between the monarch and parliaments. The judges upheld the doctrine that James I could increase customs duties without consulting parliament; they also approved Charles I's right to impose ship money, a tax that was more comprehensive and efficient than any medieval taxes; they further authorized the King's claim to have men imprisoned without showing cause, so long as he certified it was for reasons of state. James II's right to dispense with or suspend statute laws was also accepted by the High Court. In the last resort it was the King alone, not the King in Parliament, who by his prerogative was permitted to take such emergency measures as he thought fit in any time that he deemed to be a national emergency.

How far did these extensive powers or rights of the Stuart monarchy touch the life of the ordinary subject? Most of them passed him by. But the proliferation of monopolies and patents during the reign of James I caused widespread discontent, which continued to be shown in the manifestos of the Levellers, a radical group led by honest John Lilburne in the 1640s. Likewise ship money had to be paid by most of the peasantry from whom the sheriff sometimes demanded their only cow. The hearth tax was equally unpopular in the reign of Charles II. In general, taxes and other royal acts that hit the pockets of ordinary

Charles I in Council

men were the most effective sources of grievance against the Stuart monarchy. Such taxes were often imposed because of foreign wars. The idea that wars were good for trade, business, and employment, which became accepted in later times, was not generally recognized then. Most merchants agreed that war was damaging to trade, and civil war was worst of all. 'There is no greater enemy to trade than war,' wrote a merchant in 1644, 'be it in what country it will.' Henry Parker, writing on behalf of the Merchant Adventurers, condemned the 'piratical trade of war'. During the civil wars harvests were ruined, horses and cattle seized, the cloth industry severely injured. Later in the century taxes rose to unparalleled heights and men were press-

'Honest' John Lilburne

ganged into the royal navy during the long wars against France. But though economic grievances were the commonest, a substantial minority of the people were oppressed by interferences with the pursuit of their religion, stemming down from the monarch, as well as by the control exercised over their private lives by the church courts.

THE PEOPLE AND PARLIAMENT

Religion, foreign policy, and the conduct of war, together with the emergency measures necessary for its conduct, were claimed by the early Stuarts, as by the Tudors, to be the concern of the monarchy alone. But many of the political decisions which shaped the day-to-day lives of Englishmen were determined in parliament. It was parliament that voted extraordinary taxes after the monarchy had accepted that taxation by prerogative means was unconstitutional; and it was the Long Parliament of Charles II's reign that had insisted on disabilities being imposed upon nonconformists and Roman Catholics. It was this parliament too that introduced the corn laws that sent up the price of bread. Yet the parliaments of the Stuart age never represented the people as a whole.

Parliament was the preserve of the sons of the nobility and leading gentry and, to a much lesser extent, of the wealthy merchants and professional lawyers. A seat in parliament gave social prestige and offered a sounding-board for class prejudices. Hardly any of the members of the House of Commons were freely elected in the modern sense of the term. In Elizabethan times the great majority of county elections were not contested at all and the county gentry did not expect them to be contested: what they aimed at was an amicable deal between the leading local magnates. Equally there were few elections in the boroughs, where, in many cases, the franchise was even more restricted than it was in the counties. For in the counties, in theory at least, the forty-shilling freeholder, that is to say the smallest yeoman who owned his own land, had a right to vote; but in the boroughs the election was often in the hands of the local corporation, while pocket boroughs existed where a single large landowner might control all the votes. Sir John Reresby, when he became member for York at a by-election in 1674, was elected by owners of nine 'burgage' houses.

So far as was possible, then, the choice of members of parliament was decided by the local nobility, gentry, or ruling merchant class. Before the election of 1624 Lord Montagu wrote to Lord Spencer about the choice of knights of the shire for Northamptonshire that the best thing, as was the ancient practice, was to have a knight 'from the western and eastern divisions of the county—for the better service of the country, *without any opposition*'.

When writs had been issued, the King exerted what influence he could to get a group of members favourable to his own interests chosen, but he never expected to gain control of a majority in the House of Commons. Even at the general election of 1640, which resulted in the parliament that overthrew the monarchy, there is no clear evidence that electioneering in a modern sense took place or even that there were contests in the majority of the constituencies. Indeed quite a few of the nobility nominated opposition members. By the reign of Charles II Ministers who hoped to control a friendly House of Commons, like Sir Thomas Osborne, afterwards the Earl of Danby, were busily counting up the number of members holding offices or otherwise under obligations to the government who might be blackmailed, bribed or bought. Already it was recognized that many of the nobility had a group of seats more or less completely at their disposal and by the time of Queen Anne, when elections took place every three years, the groups in the House of Commons were as kaleido-scopic in character as in pre-war republican France. Parties meant little once the contest over whether or not James II should be allowed to succeed to the throne was lost by the Whigs or 'exclusionists'. But none of the nobility or gentry was particularly keen about parliamentary reform; far too many vested interests were involved; they were content to go on ruling the country by the exercise of their influence through relatives, clients, friends, or dependants. And the Crown remained happy so long as it believed it could buy up a sufficient number of influential members; then it counted on the more independent gentlemen from the counties to rally behind it, if

An election at Oxford

its cause were a good one. That was how the Queen managed to destroy the supremacy of the Whigs in 1710.

Thus, if we would understand how the political life of the English people was determined in the Stuart period, we must shut our minds to the fiercely-fought democratic general elections of our own lifetimes. Throughout most of this period fewer than half the county seats were contested at all, while two-fifths of the borough seats had only 100 electors. So the complexions of parliaments were arranged by jobbery and bribery and the representation was not of the mass of the people, but simply of the well-to-do, who understood how to manipulate the political machine for their own benefit.

Further Reading

Maurice Ashley, *England in the Seventeenth Century*, 1967
— —, *The Greatness of Oliver Cromwell*, 1962
D. Brunton and D. H. Pennington, *Members of the Long Parliament*, 1954
G. R. Cragg, *Puritanism in the Period of the Great Persecution, 1660–1688*, 1957
William Haller, *The Rise of Puritanism*, 1938
Martin J. Havran, *The Catholics in Caroline England*, 1962
Christopher Hill, *Society and Puritanism in Pre-revolutionary England*, 1964
W. G. Hoskins, *The Midland Peasant*, 1957
J. R. H. Moorman, *A History of the Church of England*, 1953
J. E. Neale, *The Elizabethan House of Commons*, 1949
H. R. Trevor-Roper, *Archbishop Laud*, 1962
Robert Walcott, *English Politics in the Early Eighteenth Century*, 1956
C. V. Wedgwood, *The King's War, 1641–1647*, 1958

VII

Education and Ideas

Even more than during the Elizabethan period the reigns of the first two Stuarts witnessed a striking advance in education. 'The evidence suggests', writes Professor W. K. Jordan, 'that this was an era of excited interest in education'; 'a period in which the vision of a new and better society enhanced by wide educational opportunities gripped men's minds'. Many grammar (or secondary) schools were founded, refounded, and expanded; vast sums of money were left by merchants and others for the support of schools; the universities were crowded with sons of gentlemen eager to learn; the educational losses caused by the destruction of the monasteries and chantries during the Protestant Reformation were more than made good.

ELEMENTARY SCHOOLS

Secondary schools expected that children who came to them about the age of eight would have already mastered reading, writing, and arithmetic and even the elements of grammar. These subjects were taught either at home or in elementary or 'petty' schools, but it is not possible to judge how many of the latter existed. Sometimes an enlightened vestry or a generous donor would start such a school or else perhaps a conscientious clergyman or public-spirited lady might begin voluntary teaching: in 1613 the Hackney vestry appointed a schoolmaster who was to take no more than 4d. a week from the parishioners for teaching their children grammar, writing, or accounts, or 2d. a week if they learned only English; in 1609

Charity school children

a lady set up a charity school at Henley on Thames to provide education in writing, reading, and casting accounts, but no grammar learning. Writing in 1660, Charles Hoole, a London schoolmaster, asserted that 'some nobler spirits whom God hath enriched with an over-plus of outward means' had erected petty school houses in their birthplaces and elsewhere, while elementary education was sometimes undertaken by 'poor women or others whose necessities compel them to undertake it'.

In addition, the grammar schools themselves occasionally formed 'petties' where an usher would teach the children to read and write. But most grammar schools, which were relatively small and usually understaffed, did not like having to do this. Dr Richard Busby, the headmaster of Westminster school in the reign of Charles II, actually gave a few pounds a year out of his own pocket to pay for the instruction of poor children of his parish. And towards the end of the seventeenth century it was becoming more widely accepted that the poor ought to receive elementary education both in order that they might carry out their work more efficiently and in order that the principles of the Christian religion should be properly instilled into them. For the purposes of reducing ignorance and irreligion in the poor a great many charity schools were founded by conscientious Anglicans in the reigns of William and Mary and Queen Anne; earlier such schools had been started by Quakers and other dissenters.

The Society for the Promotion of Christian Knowledge was particularly active in this matter: one of the original founders maintained at his own expense a school in Somerset in which no fewer than 67 boys and girls were taught their ABC, reading, writing, arithmetic tables, elementary grammar, and the New

Testament. By 1712 there were some 120 charity schools in the London area, attended by nearly 5,000 children, while another 20,000 went to schools of this kind in other parts of the country. Importance was attached to the teaching of the catechism in such schools; the boys were taught enough arithmetic to fit them to become apprentices; the girls were instructed in knitting, sewing, and spinning cloth.

It is doubtful whether primary education was widespread; for there was no spontaneous demand for it and its existence depended on an enlightened few. There is no reason to suppose

A schoolroom

that the majority of villagers were literate, but rather the contrary; and of course there were always people who said it was an error to educate the poor at all, that competent primary schoolteachers were unobtainable, and that in any case parents could not afford to pay for them. 'It is common in the mouths of many poor people', wrote Samuel Harmar in 1642, 'that if they could be free from the charge of their childrens' schooling, they would not charge the parish for their children's maintenance.' In other words, if the children stayed at home and helped with the family's work, they would be an asset and not a burden to the parish. The gentry of those days for their part certainly did not think in terms of educating the poor so that they might climb up the social ladder through the secondary schools into the universities and thence the professions. What enlightened educationists like Samuel Hartlib and John Dury had in mind was that a state-supported system of universal schooling would prevent vagrancy and crime and keep the children of the lower classes out of mischief and idleness.

So the children of the poor were apprenticed to their masters at about the age of eight when better-off children began attending the free grammar schools and private schools, which were numerous and mostly adequately endowed. The nobility rarely sent their children to such schools, but employed private tutors, usually clergymen, to teach them at home. Girls occasionally had tutors too or were taught by their mothers. And a few expensive private girls' schools are known to have flourished near London during the Stuart age. But, on the whole, the squires' daughters stayed at home, while the sons of gentlemen, merchants, and yeomen found their way into the grammar schools.

SECONDARY SCHOOLS

'The grammar school', wrote Godfrey Davies of the years 1603–60, 'attained its greatest importance during this period. It was richly supported by the middle classes which poured their wealth into endowment between 1560 and 1660, probably to a greater extent relatively than during any other hundred years in English history. The number of endowed schools founded in the first half of the seventeenth century was as large as those founded in the whole of the previous century.' The middle classes believed passionately in the virtues of education: in the grammar schools the rising classes of professional men and merchants rubbed shoulders with many of the established gentry. It has been estimated that some 1,400 grammar schools were functioning in England and Wales at this time—excluding private schools; in Norfolk alone 142 schools were counted and in Yorkshire about a hundred. Winchester and Eton were already aristocratic establishments; but such famous schools as Harrow, Rugby, Shrewsbury, Repton, Blundells, Felsted, Tonbridge and Manchester Grammar School were all prospering; in London the principal schools were Charterhouse, Christ's Hospital, Mercers, Merchant Taylors, St Paul's, and Westminster. It was clear that no town of any size was without a school. But it must be remembered that some of these numerous schools were quite small, having simply a master and an assistant and one room in which they taught. Such a school was the free grammar school at Huntingdon where Oliver Cromwell and Samuel Pepys were both educated and the premises of which, housing the new Cromwell Museum, may still be seen.

After the Restoration the grammar schools fell into disrepute, largely because they were thought to have been the nurseries of rebellion and it was feared they might become so again. Just as earlier schoolmasters with blatantly anti-Puritan sympathies were in danger of losing their posts, so after 1662 all schoolmasters who refused to conform to the new book of common

An aristocratic grammar school: Eton, c. 1675

prayer were liable to expulsion. Several schoolmasters, including the headmaster of Eton, had already lost their positions in 1660; again a number of them set up their own private schools. The nonconformists, who were especially concerned over education, not only established many schools of their own, but also academies so that boys of university age, now excluded from Oxford and Cambridge because of their religious faith, might have access to higher education of good quality for a modest fee. In general the grammar schools entered into a period of decline, partly because of losses of good teachers, partly because their ideals were out of tune with the age, and partly because of their stereotyped curricula and out-of-date statutes.

In this respect the free grammar schools were strait-jacketed from the outset. Schoolmasters required licences from bishops and were liable to fines. They were largely absorbed in instruction in Latin and divinity according to the prevailing orthodoxy of the times. To be able to talk and read Latin was the highest objective: though this was a relic of medievalism, there was the practical consideration that Latin was to some extent the commercial and diplomatic language of the civilized world. Some schools also taught a little Greek and Hebrew. Several educational critics of the seventeenth century like John Dury and Sir William Petty suggested that schoolboys might be taught to express themselves in their own native tongue or learn history, geography, and physical training. Other idealists like the political philosopher, James Harrington, wanted universal education and compulsory schools as well as a more varied selection of subjects to be taught in them. But such critics seem to have made very little impression at any rate upon the grammar schools.

Recalling his own education at Felsted in Essex (where Cromwell sent his sons), Dr John Wallis, who became Savile Professor of Geometry at Oxford, wrote:

> I . . . was pretty well acquainted with Latin and Greek tongues, having read divers authors therein (such as at schools are wont to read) and was pretty accurate in the grammars of both. . . . I had been used . . . to speak Latin. . . . I learned there somewhat

of Hebrew as to be able, with my grammar and dictionary, to proceed further without a teacher .... And I was there taught logic as a preparation to a further study at the university.

But he learned no arithmetic or other mathematics at school, and taught it himself out of books though, he said, he had 'none to direct me what book to read, or what to seek, or in what method to proceed'. He also taught himself music and French; but at the university he was soon back at Latin and Greek and the syllogisms.

Tutor and scholars

Just as in the middle of the seventeenth century enlightened critics were urging the reform of the curricula in the schools and the reduction of their obsession with Latin grammar, so later authors like John Locke and Richard Steele urged the reform of educational methods as well as subjects. It appears that often private schools were the more advanced. The father of the elder William Pitt described how his brothers learned French, accounts, drawing, dancing, and fencing at a school in Soho 'esteemed the best in England' and that he thought of sending them on to Holland later for their better education in the year 1705.

THE UNIVERSITIES

It has recently been convincingly argued by an American scholar that the higher education provided by Oxford and Cambridge in the Stuart age was more realistic and attuned to the rise of science than was once thought. Certainly the universities were beginning to attract students from all classes of the community, except the poorest, not merely would-be clerics anxious to earn a modest living. In the first decade of the seventeenth century it has been calculated that only a quarter of the students at Cambridge were men of small means. It was becoming increasingly accepted for boys from Eton and Winchester to go on to Oxford and Cambridge and for English nobility and well-to-do gentry in general to send their sons there, though most of the wealthier students appear to have been Fellow Commoners and were allowed to sit at the high tables at their colleges.

The colleges were now becoming the most important features in the organized life of the universities: that was recognized by more power being conferred on the heads of the colleges: the hebdomadal council, which included them, was established at Oxford by Charles I. Complaints were habitually made that students were idle, dissipated, and licentious, but that of course is an accusation levelled against the young in all generations, and it must be remembered that undergraduates went to universities at an earlier age than they do now. Discipline, as enforced at the universities, was pretty strict: corporal punishment for offences was not abolished until the Restoration. Undergraduates who took their degrees (not all of them did) were probably men of more learning and more highly cultivated than their predecessors a century earlier.

It is true that the university statutes tended to make the curricula look old-fashioned with their enormous emphasis on rhetoric, logic, and the classical texts. It is also suggested that lectures, even those given by professors, were poorly attended. But some college tutors were men with a remarkable breadth of outlook, who encouraged undergraduates to study the new humanities; the attacks made by the Frenchman, Peter Ramus, on Aristotle penetrated the university walls; professorships of mathematics, astronomy, and history were established by generous beneficiaries; the names of the sixteenth-century political philosophers, Machiavelli and Bodin, were not unknown. If lectures were neglected, books were read. At Oxford the Bodleian library was reorganized at the end of Elizabeth I's reign and both universities had their own printing presses.

Lord Herbert of Cherbury wrote: 'Tutors commonly spend

much time in teaching them ⌈undergraduates⌉ subtleties of logic, which, as it is usually practised, enables them for little more than to be excellent wranglers, which art, though it may be tolerable in a mercenary lawyer, I can by no means commend in a sober and well-governed gentleman.' But if logic, according to the statutes, had indeed to be the principal university subject, much extra-statutory instruction supplemented the regular studies. Modern history and modern philosophy, such as the Baconian and later the Cartesian, were recommended as suitable

Pembroke College, Oxford, founded in 1624 and named after the Chancellor of the time

subjects by college tutors. French and Italian, dancing and riding could even be learned by Oxford and Cambridge undergraduates if they wished. Scientific and mathematical studies were grafted on to the existing traditional courses. It is said that the virtuosity of the seventeenth-century English gentleman derived from the time he had spent at the university, and that Oxford and Cambridge 'provided the training that society wanted and demanded from them' (Curtis).

Nevertheless while it would be wrong to underestimate the contribution offered by universities to cultural life in England at that time it would be absurd to imagine that they resembled our modern factories of higher education and research. For one thing the physical sciences were not really taught there at all; if students wanted to study law, they naturally enrolled at the Inns of Court, though these were declining as educational institutions by the reign of Charles II. Much depended on the character and quality of the college tutors who were not at all well paid. Dr William Taswell, who became a professor of Greek, would have done better financially when he was a young Fellow at Oxford to accept the posts offered him as a schoolmaster or a private tutor in a nobleman's household. Research was not then reckoned to be a function of the universities at all and far more intellectual progress was achieved in the Royal Society once it was established in London in 1660 than either at Oxford or Cambridge.

In the Stuart period Oxford was recognized as being the older, more distinguished, and more conservative of the two universities. Two new colleges, Pembroke and Wadham, were opened early in the seventeenth century. Cambridge was more puritanical, Emmanuel and Sidney Sussex being notorious as hotbeds of dissent. Samuel Ward, Master of Sidney Sussex, was one of the leading opponents of the idea of free will. Colleges both at Oxford and Cambridge were loyal to Charles I and offered money and plate towards his funds when war came, although Oliver Cromwell stopped much of the plate from leaving Cambridge. Oxford became the residence of the royal Court and the headquarters of the Royalist army. The government,

Emmanuel College, Cambridge: chapel, gallery and loggias, designed by Wren, 1668–77

although contributing little by way of money, always commanded influence over the universities. The first Duke of Buckingham, favourite of the first two Stuart kings, got his friends appointed college Fellows; the Cromwells, when they were in power, were both Chancellors of Oxford and had their own cronies. The monarchs selected the Chancellors and through them were able to influence appointments to colleges. When a tremendous row developed during the reign of James II because he tried to get his creatures appointed to headships of colleges at both universities he was in fact only trying to exercise powers which had been successfully exercised without provoking protest, by his predecessors.

THE GROWTH OF SCIENCE

Although science was not yet officially studied in the universities, the seventeenth century in England saw a remarkable advance in scientific ideas which was ultimately to have its impact on the life of the English people. A. N. Whitehead described it as 'a century of genius' and recently an American scholar has spoken of 'the leadership that England held in the development of science at the time' (Richard S. Westfall). But, as always, the scientific revolution was international. After the invention of printing, the telescope, and the compass men everywhere became conscious of new concepts displacing the revered teachings of Greece and Rome. There was an interchange of ideas across the frontiers. For example, the famous English doctor and anatomist, William Harvey had studied under Galileo Galilei at the university of Padua, where the medical teaching was the best in the world, while Galileo anticipated Sir Isaac Newton's first two laws of motion. During the century Huygens in Holland, Descartes in France, and Leibniz in Germany all contributed to the progress of mathematics and physics. Gradually 'natural philosophy' or pure science extricated itself from the trammels of Aristotle, Galen, and Ptolemy.

In recent years it has been fashionable to depreciate the contribution made to this forward sweep by Francis Bacon, Vis-

Francis Bacon (1561–1620)

count St Albans, who was James I's Lord Chancellor. It is said that he did not understand the true nature of scientific methods and that his influence has been exaggerated. Bacon advocated empiricism, utilitarianism, and induction. He also preached the doctrine that the purpose of science was to gain power over nature. In his *Novum Organum* (1620) he wrote: 'Human knowledge and human power are one; for where the cause is not known, the effect cannot be produced. Nature to be commanded must be obeyed; and that which is in contemplation is as the cause is in operation as the rule.' Bacon stressed the importance of experiments and hoped that out of them some broad principles and valuable discoveries would emerge. But it has been pointed out that the inductive process by itself leads nowhere; experiments must be organized in relation to a specific concept; there has never been natural science with no preconceived ideas about theoretical objectives. It is asserted that Bacon's teachings had little immediate effect except in Oxford and that in any case in his insistence upon experimentation he had already been anticipated by many others at home and abroad.

The impulses towards scientific study were numerous. They were economic, social, even religious: some scientists were actually disinterested seekers after truth. Robert Boyle, himself a disinterested scientist and 'the father of modern chemistry' wrote an immense book in the 1660s entitled *The Usefulness of Experimental Natural Philosophy*. Others thought of themselves as justifying the ways of God to man. Francis Bacon and, to a lesser extent, Isaac Newton were optimistic about the speed with which scientists would conquer nature, and they were not wrong in thinking that the fecundity of ideas in their times was

132

far greater than ever before in English history. Whatever the defects of Bacon's thinking and his own failures in experimenting, his exhortations did have considerable impact. Boyle confessed himself to be a pupil of Bacon; Robert Hooke, an able mathematician and astronomer, employed Bacon's methods; William Harvey acknowledged his personal debt to Bacon; and the founders of the Royal Society were profoundly moved by Bacon's belief that the scientist could wield power over nature in the service of humanity. And whatever may have been wrong over Bacon's emphasis on experiments, it is interesting that Newton wrote in 1672: 'The best and safest method of philosophizing seems to be, first diligently to investigate the properties of things and establish them by experiment, and then to seek hypotheses to explain them.'

The early members of the Royal Society were devoted would-be technologists. Inspired by Baconian precepts, they fancied that inventions that would enrich the welfare of the English people might be completed almost over night. The Royal Society grew out of a group of thinkers who met for discussions on scientific matters at Oxford towards the end of the Interregnum. One of their leading spirits was Dr John Wilkins, Warden of Wadham, an amateur astronomer who became the first secretary of the Society when it was established in London.

Astronomy: the observing-room at Greenwich

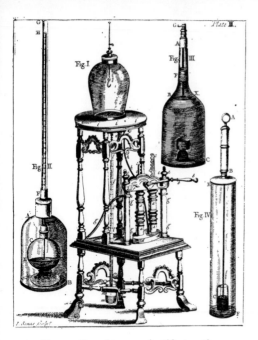

Pneumatics: from a scientific treatise

It received a royal charter in July, 1662. King Charles II and his cousin, Prince Rupert, were enthusiastic amateur scientists and many of the original members of the Society were dilettantes. For example, there was Sir Kenelm Digby who had invented a 'powder of sympathy' (sulphate of iron dissolved in water) that would 'heal in a very short time all kinds of hurts that are not mortal'. However, other more genuine scientists or philosophers like Harvey, Boyle, Hooke, Newton, John Locke and Thomas Sydenham joined the Society and were stimulated by each other's flow of ideas. Amateurs like John Evelyn soon tired of it and the progress of scientific thought and discovery was interrupted by plague, fire, and war. 'By 1680', writes Sir George Clark, 'the Society was at a low ebb. In the following years there was something of a revival. But the Society's work on industrial science took only a modest place in the proceedings.'

Attempts made to interest this group of scientists in practical problems of transport, naval engineering, agricultural improvement, and medical research petered out. The Royal College of Physicians is said to have been so perturbed lest the Royal Society should interfere with its prerogatives that a pamphleteer was hired to attack it. Though for the time being the Society was the lively centre of talk and inquiry it tried too hard over too broad a field that ranged from tin-mining to English grammar and from statistics to bee-keeping. The great scientific discoveries of the latter half of the Stuart age were chiefly theoretical, as in Newtonian physics, and were achieved by individuals moved by the restless spirit of the time. Indeed

Newton himself was a rather lonely figure; and in spite of the immense range of his mathematical discoveries he largely abandoned science in his later life. Boyle, who died in 1691, foresaw that chemistry would transform both agriculture and medicine. But nothing much emerged for another century.

In so far as there were technological advances, they came up against much public resistance. Reference has been made earlier to the rioting in London against new inventions, for example, in silk-weaving. Saw-mills had to stop working in 1663; stocking-frames were smashed in 1710. Daniel Defoe argued against the introduction of labour-saving devices on the ground that: ''Tis the excellence of our English manufacture that it is so planned to go through as many hands as possible; he that contrives to have it go through fewer ought at the same time to provide work for the rest.' This is a sentiment that would meet with approval from many modern trade unionists. But in any case co-operation between science and industry was unknown in the Stuart period.

SCIENCE AND RELIGION

Whether the 'virtuosity' of the English gentleman of Stuart times was inspired by the aphorisms of Francis Bacon, by the initial enthusiasms of the Royal Society, or, as has lately been claimed, by the extra-curricular activity at Oxford and Cambridge, the fact remains that the theories of utilitarianism, which found their supreme expressions in the writings of John Locke and the mechanical explanations of natural phenomena, which were generally accepted not only among the natural scientists but among the latter-day theologians, affected the thinking of educated men in general.

Unquestionably the notable scientific discoveries that gradually penetrated into English society had a profound impact upon Christian beliefs. Yet the leading members of the Royal Society would have hesitated to admit this. Dr John Wilkins, its first secretary, thought that astronomy lit up the glory of God. 'It proved God and a providence,' he wrote, 'and incites our hearts to a greater admiration and fear of His omnipotency. We may

Sir Isaac Newton (1642-1727)

understand by the heavens how much mightier He is that made them.' Robert Boyle, who was virtually a Puritan, having experienced 'conversion', and lived a life of piety and moral restraint, called himself 'the Christian Virtuoso' and argued that God had created the universe to display his own glory and was anxious that it should be fully understood how it worked. John Ray, the naturalist, wrote a book entitled *The Wisdom of God Manifested in the Works of Creation* which aimed to demonstrate the skill and wisdom of the Almighty. And Sir Isaac Newton, who devoted much of his life to the study of theology (there are ten different versions of one of his theological treatises) had no doubt at all about the basic harmony of science and religion. In a letter written in 1692 Newton said: 'When I wrote my treatise about my system [*The Principia*] I had an eye upon such principles as might work with considering men for the belief of a deity; and nothing can rejoice me more than to find it useful for that purpose.'

But the trouble was that 'considering men', whatever they might have thought about the laws of gravitation or the wonders of nature as evidence for the existence of God, were increasingly becoming aware that the Bible, or at any rate the Old Testament, could hardly be literally true. While Dr Wilkins was able to calculate that there would have been room for all the animals in Noah's ark, Samuel Pepys noted in 1684 that: 'Noah's Ark must needs be made of some extraordinary timber and plank, that could remain good after having been a hundred years in building, whereas our thirty new ships are rotten within less than five. Moreover Mr Sheres computes from its dimensions that six months would have sufficed to have built what Moses assigns an hundred years for.'

Some writers have claimed that Puritanism contributed markedly to the evolution of the scientific spirit; others have pointed out with equal justice that men like Galileo, Descartes, and Pascal were all Roman Catholics. The fact is that the rapid development of mechanical theories was characteristic of the age and was not related to any one particular religious tendency. Most of the chief physical scientists were Christians. Yet other Christian leaders were growing perturbed over whither their theories were taking them. Richard Baxter, the eminent Puritan divine, thought that the temper of scientific research, which he deemed Epicurean, endangered the very foundations of Christianity; Robert Boyle thought it wise to bequeath money to establish lectures in defence of religion; Sir Thomas Browne, himself a doctor, published a personal apologia for religion in a scientific age.

The fact is that throughout the Stuart period, though most thinkers and authors used a religious terminology and continued to pay respect to the omnipotence of God as He revealed Himself in nature, they were little agreed about what they meant by religion. To give two instances of this among really great writers: John Milton, usually thought of as the supreme Puritan poet, came to disbelieve in the doctrine of predestination, questioned some of the biblical teachings, and did not accept the immortality of the soul. John Locke, the philosopher most admired in the reigns of King William III and Queen Anne, did not credit the divinity of Jesus Christ and, though he published a book called *The Reasonableness of Christianity*, was afterwards accused with some plausibility of being an atheist.

The most doubtful Christian of the Stuart age, Thomas Hobbes the political philosopher, was not a member of the Royal Society and while he wrote perhaps the ablest book on political theory of the century, *The Leviathan* (1651) was largely ignored by Locke and other philosophers because of his shocking religious and moral opinions. Not that he was entirely ignored, for his acute mind was undoubtedly feared. Dr John Wallis, the mathematician (Hobbes thought of himself as a mathematician, although he was an indifferent one) observed 'Our Leviathan is furiously attacking and destroying our universities (and not only ours but all) and especially ministers and the clergy and all religion'. Indeed it was scientists like Wallis and

Boyle who were the most notable defenders of Christianity when the philosophers were beginning to undermine it. By the reign of Queen Anne both the Puritan belief in the literal interpretation of the Bible and the High Church faith in the miracles of Christianity had sustained heavy blows. But the official Church began to adapt itself. Though Queen Anne herself was a supporter of the High Church, the restrained and tolerant concepts of the 'rational' theologians or 'latitudinarian' churchmen were beginning to penetrate the whole of English society at the top. At the bottom no doubt superstitious and ritualistic beliefs still prevailed. 'It was lucky for the witches', wrote Dr Trevelyan of that reign, 'that England was still aristocratically governed.' For it was the judges and not the juries who ensured that alleged witches were no longer put to death, as they had been in large numbers a century earlier; it was the bishops who were ceasing to believe in fairies, though they have been believed in by scientists right down to modern times.

Thomas Hobbes's masterpiece

Thus, though popular rage might still demand that witches should be put to death, though a London mob might be found to cheer for a reactionary cleric in the reign of Queen Anne, though in the countryside rural superstitions might still persist largely unchanged, and though natural philosophy had still failed to provide improvements in transport, agriculture or medicine, new ideas were beginning to move the minds of educated Englishmen. As Bertrand Russell has written:

At the beginning of the [seventeenth] century Sir Thomas Browne took part in trials for witchcraft; at the end such a thing would have been impossible. In Shakespeare's time comets were still portents; after the publication of Newton's *Principia* in 1687, it was known that he and Halley had calculated the orbits of certain com-

Lingering superstition: 'swimming' a witch

ets, and that they were as obedient as the planets to the laws of gravitation. The reign of law had established its hold on men's imaginations, making such things as magic and sorcery incredible. In 1700 the mental outlook of educated men was completely modern. . . .

That was indeed the outstanding historical transformation in the Stuart age; but, as has been said, it was a penetration that took place only at the top. This change in outlook was not to have much effect on men's way of living for many years.

Further Reading

J. W. Adamson, *A Short History of Education*, 1922
G. N. Clark, *Science and Social Welfare in the Age of Newton*, 1937
A. C. Crombie, *Augustine to Galileo*, 1957
Mark H. Curtis, *Oxford and Cambridge in Transition*, 1959
Bertrand Russell, *A History of Western Philosophy*, 1946
W. A. L. Vincent, *The State and School Education, 1640–1660*, 1950
Richard S. Westfall, *Science and Religion in Seventeenth Century England*, 1958

VIII

Arts and Letters

THE THEATRE

The modern theatre had come into being in the reign of Queen Elizabeth I when large audiences appreciated fine acting and ingeniously contrived plays enlivened by music, dance and song. James I proved to be a more generous patron of the arts than his predecessor. When he came to London six theatres were in existence there, of which the more important were the Globe, the Fortune, and the Curtain. Eight days after he arrived he took over by Letters Patent the company previously known as the Lord Chamberlain's Men:

> Know ye that We . . . have licensed . . . these our servants, Lawrence Fletcher, William Shakespeare, Richard Burbage etc. . . . freely to use and exercise the art and faculty of playing . . . as well for the recreation of our loving subjects as for Our solace and pleasure when we shall think good to see them.

Shakespeare was the greatest playwright of the time, Burbage the greatest actor. Of the latter a poet wrote when he died:

> *Oft have I seen him play this part in jest*
> *So lively that spectators and the rest*
> *Of his sad crew, whilst he but seemed to bleed,*
> *Amazed, thought even then he died in deed.*

By the end of 1603 two other theatrical companies had been taken over by the Court. During the period of the Court 'revels', which usually lasted well beyond the twelve days after Christmas, Shakespeare and his fellow actors would be entertaining

Whitehall: not only Shakespeare's comedies and tragedies but the plays of Ben Jonson, Massinger, Beaumont and Fletcher and other dramatists of the time were frequently performed before the King and Queen. Soon James's Queen, who was even more enthusiastic than her husband about plays, had exhausted their entire repertoire.

London in the early days of James I's reign retained much of its Elizabethan artistic glories. Beaumont and Fletcher, Inigo Jones, to become famous as an architect, Ben Jonson, John Donne, and Michael Drayton, an older poet, and, it is believed, Shakespeare himself used to forgather at a club held in the Mermaid Tavern off Cheapside to exchange ideas. Beaumont wrote:

> *What things we have seen*
> *Done at the Mermaid! Heard words that have been*
> *So nimble and so full of subtle flame,*
> *As if that every one from whence they came*
> *Had meant to put his whole wit in a jest*
> *And had resolved to live a fool the rest*
> *Of his dull life. . . .*

Five other theatres were built during the reign, including the Phoenix in Drury Lane, one of the first indoor theatres. But theatres open to the general public suffered ups-and-downs because they had automatically to be closed during the plagues. Then the companies would tour the provinces as far north as the Midlands or perform for the benefit of the Court or nobility in private houses, as for example at Wilton near Salisbury, the home of the Earl of Pembroke. Once the King's Men travelled all the way from Mortlake in Surrey to Wilton where they gave a performance of *As you Like It* for the amusement of their monarch who rewarded them with £30 for their trouble.

Not only did the Court patronize such professional companies but it also expended large

Design for a masque by Inigo Jones

A 'Droll' at the Red Bull playhouse

sums on the masques that were performed in splendour by society amateurs. Inigo Jones was much concerned with the presentation of these masques: he designed magnificent costumes and elaborate scenery and introduced the proscenium arch and coloured lights. In that way these private theatricals began to rival and to influence technically the old-fashioned outdoor theatre that had been enjoyed by the groundlings in Elizabethan times. It is thought that the plot of *The Tempest*, Shakespeare's last play, with its provision for special dramatic effects, may have been affected by these novel devices. The small Blackfriars theatre, which Shakespeare's company leased in 1608 for winter performances, was one of the early indoor theatres, though it is doubtful whether it employed much scenery. As late as 1640 theatre companies were apologizing for the absence of scenery: the producer of *The Country Captain*, performed in that year, said bitingly in introducing it:

> *Gallants, I'll tell you what we do not mean*
> *To show you here—a glorious painted scene*
> *With various doors to stand instead of wit*
> *Or richer clothes of lace for lines well writ.*

Yet in the reign of Charles I, who, with his French wife, was a keen lover of masques, the theatre had become more and more the plaything of the court and the nobility and less and less a public entertainment. 'An age of gallantry and aristocratic splendour', wrote Allardyce Nicoll, 'was rapidly coming to the

142

theatre.' In fact, with the passing of Shakespeare and Burbage and the burning down of the first Globe theatre a magnificent era had ended.

The Puritans condemned the theatre as immoral; ordinances of 1642 and 1647 closed the theatres and actors were liable to be prosecuted as rogues. Nevertheless there were a number of private performances during the Interregnum, Oliver Cromwell was a patron of music, and the first English opera, *The Siege of Rhodes,* was performed with official permission in 1656. Sir William Davenant, who produced the opera, was reputedly an illegitimate son of Shakespeare, thus linking the early and later Stuart theatre. His was one of the two principal companies licensed after the Restoration and known as the Duke's Men; the other company was again called the King's Men. The Duke's Men first performed in Lincoln's Inn Fields and later in Dorset Garden. The Theatre Royal, Drury Lane, opened in 1674, had provision for scenery and other mechanical devices. In these London theatres actresses began to perform for the first time and that further stimulated the interest and the patronage of the King and the Duke of York, who were both connoisseurs of the opposite sex.

Thus for a time the English theatre became modern, professional, and subject to enthusiastic royal patronage. The wandering players and acrobats, who had often been treated as vagabonds as they ploughed their way from inn to inn, began to bathe in the reflected light of an acting tradition that stretched from Burbage and Edward Alleyn (the founder of Dulwich College) to Thomas Betterton and Nell Gwyn. Anyone who wanted to be in the

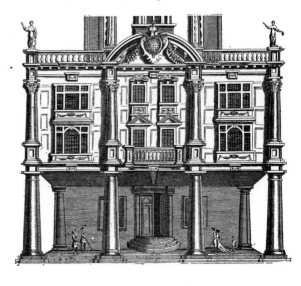

The Duke's Theatre, built in 1662

Nell Gwyn (1650–87)

social swing, as Samuel Pepys did, simply had to go to the theatre where a host of dramatists, from John Dryden, the poet laureate who succeeded Davenant, to William Congreve, met the needs of the aristocratic audiences of their time. But these high society audiences were ill behaved:

> *One half of the play they spend in*
> *noise and brawl,*
> *Sleep out the rest, then wake and*
> *damn it all.*

Because the theatre had become too completely the amusement of the few, it nearly faded away. The fashionable audiences proved insufficient to support two theatres in the capital: in 1682 the King's company and the Duke's were amalgamated while 'except for several strolling companies and for visits of the London companies to Oxford and Cambridge plays were unknown' (Nicoll). After the death of Charles II and the exile of his brother the accession to the throne of two Stuart Queens generated an atmosphere of royal piety which had a chastening effect on the stage. The general drive for the improvement of manners and morals put an end to the taste for those blood-curdling dramas and lascivious comedies that had flourished after the bright summer morning of the Restoration. Even Shakespeare was considered too daring and had to be edited. Congreve's *Way of the World* (produced in 1700) was the swan song of the older tradition in comedy. It even appeared as if the theatre was dying at the time the novel was coming into being.

POETRY AND PROSE

Actors needed patrons: and they obtained modest patrons either from the general public who sat in the galleries of the London theatres or from the tipplers in the alehouses and inns who cast coins to strolling players, while they also received patronage

144

from the aristocracy who invited companies to perform in their
stately homes and from the Stuart monarchs who brought their
own companies to Whitehall Palace. But for the authors of
those days it was rather less easy. That is why it has been said,
for instance, that 'the English lyric never had such a popular
life as the English drama'. In so far as lyrical poetry was
popular it was in song, as with the medieval minstrels. When
Suckling wrote:

> *Why so pale and wan, fond lover?*
> *Prithee why so pale?*

Or Herrick:

> *Gather ye rosebuds while ye may*
> *Old time is still a-flying:*
> *And this same flower that smiles today*
> *Tomorrow will be dying.*

they were writing within the framework of traditional song.
Even John Milton, in one of his earliest verses (written when
he was 15) gave those who were to be his fellow Puritans
something to sing about, if they wished:

> *Let us, with gladsome mind,*
> *Praise the Lord, for he is kind:*
> *For his mercies aye endure,*
> *Ever faithful, ever sure.*

That was from his rhymed version of the 136th Psalm.

But most poets, if they were not writing merely for their
fellows or to please themselves (that must sometimes have
happened: many of John Donne's poems were not published
until after he was dead), were dependent on patrons of one kind
or another. It was customary for authors to seek noble patrons:
hence the eulogistic dedications, as the mysterious dedication
of Shakespeare's sonnets to 'W.H.', although it was not
composed by Shakespeare but by an unscrupulous bookseller
engaged in pirating the poet's work. Sometimes subscription
lists for books, notably for translations of classics, were opened;
political satires might be subsidized; with good luck the patronage of the King might be gained for writers, as for artists.

Printers at work, c. 1710

James I, who was, or liked to think of himself as, a learned man and was the only Stuart king to write books himself, was not averse from conferring patronage on authors. Finally, booksellers, who believed that they could dispose of a reasonable number of copies of a book or a pamphlet, would be willing to give authors a very modest lump sum for them—though they, like modern publishers, were never noted for excessive generosity: nor was being an author (unless one were an amateur) thought to be especially high-class under the Stuarts, any more than it is today.

In so far as there was a ready-made readership available in the seventeenth century it was certainly not for great literature but for controversial political and theological pamphlets, which, as we know from the collections of the bookseller, George Thomason, were produced in vast numbers in the middle of the century, or later for fictional entertainment, such as the romances of Aphra Behn, the first English woman novelist, or for the scurrilous journalism of a Ned Ward or the imaginative reporting of a Daniel Defoe. On the eve of the civil wars there was a heavy output of polemical literature by both sides who thought it worth while to battle it out with their pens before taking to their swords. Much later in the reign of Queen Anne Defoe, Swift, and Addison entered the lists of political pamphleteers hired in the cause of party. But at the same time patronage was available for good literature, otherwise the remarkable list of seventeenth-century English authors which can so quickly be compiled would scarcely exist. 'There were in fact a great many students [of literature] among the upper and middle classes both of town and country', wrote Dr. Trevelyan of this time. Cultivated ladies like the Duchess of Newcastle and

146

Dorothy Osborne were book readers. So were a number of country gentlemen, when not out hunting, and even yeomen, such as Adam Eyre the Yorkshireman who noted more than once in his diary: 'This day I rested at home and spent most of the day reading', although how far he was typical is not clear. At any rate, books had to be bought at shops, for there were no lending libraries: most manor houses boasted a bookshelf or two and noblemen's houses had their libraries. Towards the end of the Stuart period newspapers came into existence, and literary journalism then began to stimulate the reading of books.

The Puritans were prolific writers and, to judge by the pamphlets and sermons, they must have been voracious readers too. The Authorized Version of the Bible, published in 1612, afforded a stimulus to their kind of writing, but most poets were individualists. The four most famous prose writers of the earlier Stuart age—Francis Bacon, Walter Raleigh, Richard Burton, and Thomas Browne—were all quite different, not only in their subjects but their styles. The two most celebrated Puritan authors wrote their finest works after Puritanism had been driven underground—John Milton and John Bunyan—one majestically classical, the other instinct with the vivid humour and indomitable optimism of an ordinary convert.

But, on the whole, literary men did not deliberately set out to portray the life of their times, as did the historians and diarists. One reads Shakespeare or Ben Jonson, Donne or Herbert, Milton or Dryden for the pleasure that they give us outside the context of their period. If one wants to know what went on then one turns to Pepys's diary or Clarendon's *History of the Rebellion* or the numerous letters that have survived in country houses or public archives, such as those of John Chamberlain or Anne Conway or dozens of others lovingly preserved and edited. But artists of genius can be fitted into no category. It does not matter much whether the poets belonged to the 'Tribe' of Ben Jonson or to the 'Metaphysicals'. Even the Puritans are hard to pin down: for instance, Milton, usually considered the supreme Puritan poet, wrote his masque *Comus* for performance in the house of a nobleman the year after

John Dryden (1631-1700)

William Prynne had published his *Histriomastix* condemning in the name of Puritanism all masques as immoral. And, again, Milton's earliest poems are difficult to distinguish from those of the contemporary royalist lyricists. The ablest satirist who wrote during the reign of Charles II was Andrew Marvell, who had served under Milton in Oliver Cromwell's Protectorate, and not Samuel Butler, who made his name by mocking the Puritans in his *Hudibras*. John Dryden, another satirist, whose plays were typical of much Restoration drama, was to die a pious Roman Catholic, and some think his *Hind and the Panther*, a plea for his Church, to be the best of his long poems. Dryden was not only a great poet but a notable literary critic in an age when, as James Sutherland has said, 'gentlemen took to writing songs, epigrams, satires, and plays as they have never done before or since'. So the gentlemen of England read, wrote, and criticized one another's work. At the end of the Stuart age Dean Swift drew attention to Dryden's criticisms in his prefaces:

> *Read all the Prefaces of Dryden*
> *For these our Criticks much confide in*
> *(Tho' meerly writ at first for filling*
> *To raise the Volume's Price, a Shilling).*

Thus all these authors of genius, from William Shakespeare to Jonathan Swift, who spanned the long century that constitutes the Stuart era, could command readership and patronage: that in itself is a tribute to the culture and taste of their wonderful age.

ARCHITECTURE

If men of letters needed a variety of patrons, English architecture relied much on the direct support of the Court, for the

two outstanding men who bestrode their times were both
Surveyors of the King's Works: Inigo Jones, who lived from
1573 until 1652, and Christopher Wren, who was born in 1632
and died in 1723, having lived long enough to become a back
number. Neither of these men was a trained professional
architect. Jones was the son of a clothworker at Smithfield and
a self-made man, who first earned a reputation at Court as the
ingenious stage manager of the royal masques. As has been
observed, the elaborate scenery, costumes, and mechanical
devices used in these entertainments made their impact upon
the English theatre. A clever, ambitious, domineering man,
Inigo Jones and the expansive Ben Jonson, working together,
were outstanding favourites as masque-makers at James I's
Court. Eventually they quarrelled when Jonson wrote *The Tale
of the Tub*, a play in which he held Inigo Jones up to ridicule in
his character Vitruvius Hoope. In that play Jonson makes him
say:

> I have a little knowledge in design
> Which I can vary, Sir, to *Infinito*

Tub. Ad infinitum, Sir, you mean.

> I do.
> I stand not on my Latin, I'll invent
> But I must be alone then, joined with no man

That was a clear enough commentary on Jones's character.

Twice Jones visited Italy, once in the company of Thomas
Howard, second Earl of Arundel, one of those maligned
Howards of James I's reign, who was a genuine patron of the
arts. Jones was deeply influenced by Palladio and by the Italian
Renaissance architecture. It was his influence that contributed
much to the decline of 'Tudor Gothic'. After being Surveyor
to Prince Henry, he was promoted to be Surveyor to the King
in 1615 when he was 42. The Surveyor's duty was to advise
the King on all matters relating to building and to approve or
design buildings for royalty. Two of his most famous buildings
were the Queen's House at Greenwich and the Banqueting
House at Whitehall, but there is much controversy over the

Inigo Jones's masterpiece: the banqueting house, Whitehall, 1619–22

rest of his work. He is known to have designed a magnificent portico for the old St Paul's cathedral, which was destroyed in the Great Fire, and also to have built St Paul's church in Covent Garden which was burnt down in 1795. He also designed the first Temple Bar, a magnificent gateway between the Strand and Fleet Street. Jones ceased to be Surveyor in 1642 and died still a wealthy man in 1652, for the post was rich in pickings.

Wren was a step up the social scale from Inigo Jones, for his father was a clergyman. But like Jones, he did not first earn his reputation as an architect. Beginning as a scientist, by the age of 25 he was a professor of astronomy at Gresham College in London. Not only was he concerned with the telescope, but he was something of a mathematician, physiologist, meteorologist, and inventor: among his ingenuities was a pen designed to copy manuscripts in duplicate. A prominent figure in the Royal Society and from 1661 Professor of Astronomy at Oxford, Wren's knack as an architect was illustrated by an offer from Charles II to send him as a surveyor to Tangier, which was acquired when the King married a Portuguese princess in 1662. But Wren's big opportunity came when Gilbert Sheldon,

Bishop of London, undertook to endow a university building at Oxford: Wren designed the Sheldonian theatre, which still survives. That was completed in 1669, and in the same year Wren was preferred over two other candidates as the King's Surveyor. Already he had impressed the Court with his plan for rebuilding London after the Great Fire, to which are directly owing Wren's City churches and the new St Paul's cathedral that replaced the dilapidated building adorned with Inigo Jones's front.

Wren was influenced by the Italian architects, Bramante and Bernini. Bernini he met briefly during a visit to Paris when he was excited by the Louvre and to a lesser extent by Versailles. Yet he does not appear to have been much indebted to his predecessor, Inigo Jones, although both of them worked in the Italian Renaissance tradition. Even today modern architectural critics are not agreed on their relative merits. We have the advantage of knowing more about Wren and what he stood for. He once wrote that 'always the true test is natural or geometrical

The Sheldonian Theatre, Oxford, by Sir Christopher Wren, 1664–9

A Wren City church: St Mary-le-Bow, 1671–80

beauty' and it has been observed that the secret of his work was its eloquence and precision. Towards the end of his life there was a comic argument over whether a balustrade, as in Inigo Jones's Banqueting House, should be added to Wren's St Paul's. Wren did not want it and complained that '*ladies* think nothing well without an edging'. However, the balustrade was added.

Other famous architects of the century were Jones's followers, John Webb, designer of Greenwich Palace, and Roger Pratt, designer of Clarendon House. Wren was succeeded by the Palladians, Nicholas Hawksmoor, who built All Souls College, Oxford, and James Gibbs, who built the church of St Martin-in-the-Fields, London, soon after Wren's death. The Marlboroughs preferred the eccentric John Vanbrugh to design Blenheim Palace, though afterwards they regretted it, and the Duchess employed Wren to build Marlborough House in London. Thus the historic beauties of London architecture derived much from the Stuart age.

PAINTING AND SCULPTURE

Like architecture, painting was indebted to the patronage of the Court and the wealthier nobility. But painting was to that age much what photography is to our own. The gentry liked to buy paintings of their families and often ordered more than one copy. The rich patronized the fashionable painters, many of whom were of foreign origin, such as Anthony Van Dyck, Peter Lely, and Godfrey Kneller. Charles I and Charles II both encouraged talent from abroad, and few English artists equalled the best of them. Charles I was a discerning patron of the arts and built up a fine collection of Italian and Flemish masterpieces. Noblemen like Arundel, the eleventh earl of Shrewsbury, and the first Earl of Clarendon were also collectors. Prince Rupert, Charles I's nephew, loved engravings and himself demonstrated the technique of the mezzotint.

There were a large number of English portrait painters and miniaturists, although practically no landscape artists. William Dobson was the best

William Dobson (1610–46)

of the portrait painters—he was the great painter of the civil war days at Oxford, but died in poverty—and Samuel Cooper was the finest miniaturist. There were plenty of others: the inferior Robert Walker did a roaring trade during the Interregnum: Mrs Oliver Cromwell once ordered three copies of his painting of her husband to be distributed among his friends.

Sculpture, like architecture, was influenced by Italy: men like Pierce and Bushnell were competent enough at producing portrait busts and Grinling Gibbons was a celebrated wood engraver. But many of the artists employed by the Court were foreign, ranging from Wenceslaus Hollar, the Bohemian engraver, to Antonio Verrio, the Italian painter and decorator. Le Sueur who created the statue of Charles I on horseback was a Frenchman. It was perhaps symptomatic that, on the whole, Cromwell lent his patronage to English artists and Charles II to French ones. But reflecting, as they did, the general European transition from Gothic to Baroque, it can be said that the visual arts in the Stuart age experienced a historical turning point.

An artist at work

153

MUSIC

Music has always been one of the most popular of the arts, stretching across the years from the singing of medieval part-songs to the performance of present-day 'pop' music. At the beginning of the Stuart period the popularity of madrigals and 'ayres' was coming to an end, but the singing of secular songs outside church and of sacred songs inside sustained the native musical tradition. Again the Court was the focus of patronage: the masques needed their musicians as well as their poets and stage designers, and composers like William and Henry Lawes and Matthew Locke received encouragement for that reason. Milton wrote of Henry Lawes:

> *Harry, whose tuneful and well-measur'd song*
> *First taught our English music how to span*
> *Words with just note and accent, not to scan*
> *With Midas's ears, committing short and long.*

However a modern critic affirms that Lawes, though certainly one of the most successful song-writers of his time, did not depart in any revolutionary way from old English traditions.

Henry Purcell, possibly the greatest and most versatile English composer of all time, who lived from 1659 to 1695, was born in the Court and received its patronage, becoming the organist at Westminster Abbey. During the latter half of the seventeenth century the first public concerts were given and the first operas performed. Once again art was essentially international. Charles II admired the Italian Lully; in Queen Anne's reign the German Handel visited London to produce the first Italian operas. Purcell himself blended Italian and French styles with the English traditions.

Choristers

Music was then part of the education

Playing the flageolet

of English gentlemen and gentlewomen. One can observe something of the popularity of music in the middle classes in the life of Samuel Pepys, who was a friend of Purcell's father. Pepys loved to sing songs, play instruments— lute, viol, violin, flageolet— and even tried his hand at composition. He took lessons in music, while he allowed his wife to be taught singing and dancing. Music, he claimed, was 'the thing of the world I love most' and he tried hard to stimulate his wife's interest in it. Though she proved to be no song-stress, she mastered the flageolet. When long after he gave up keeping his diary owing to his failing eyesight and his wife had died, Pepys sailed to Tangier in 1683, one of the pleasures that he anticipated on the voyage was that 'of concerts (much above the ordinary) of voices, flutes, and violins'. Music and dancing were in fact the solace of all classes. Music enlivened the theatres and the alehouses; dancing rejoiced alike the Court and the village green. Whereas architecture and sculpture were the gratifications of the rich, and painting was the flattering photography of the upper and middle classes, these two arts were the joy of all people, as they still are today.

Further Reading

Frederick Bridge, *Samuel Pepys, Lover of Musique*, 1903
Boris Ford (ed.), *From Donne to Marvell*, 1962
J. Alfred Gotch, *Inigo Jones* (illustrated), 1928
F. E. Halliday, *The Life of Shakespeare* (illustrated), 1961
Allardyce Nicoll, *The English Theatre: A Short History*, 1938
— —, *A History of English Drama, 1660–1700*, 1952
Peter Quennell, *Shakespeare*, 1963
John Summerson, *Sir Christopher Wren* (illustrated), 1953
Ernest Walker, *A History of Music in England*, 1924

C. V. Wedgwood, *Seventeenth Century English Literature*, 1950

Margaret Whinney and Oliver Millar, *English Art, 1625–1714* (illustrated), 1950

IX

Travel and Adventure

TRAVEL AT HOME

The roads in Stuart England, though infinitely less dangerous to ride along than they are today, were much less comfortable. Two main changes had taken place since the Elizabethan period; the first was that, since more of the country was enclosed for agricultural purposes, more hedgerows and fences were appearing, and thus the traveller, if forced off the customary tracks on account of their bad condition, found it less easy than before to make his way across private fields, treading down the crops as he went; secondly, there was more wheeled traffic about. The medieval roads, which were little more than rights of way, were not intended for heavy wheel barrows, let alone 'flying coaches', and on their unlaid and undressed surfaces the wheel ruts became rivulets in the winter and dry ditches in the summer.

It was, as has been seen, the duty of the parish surveyors of the highways to keep the main roads clear, while the by-ways were the responsibility of the landowners through whose properties they passed. Some conscientious surveyors existed, but since they could call out workers for only six days in the year and could not pay them, as a rule very little got done; even the cutting down of hedges by the roadside or the scouring of ditches was often neglected. Well-to-do people would give tips to the local road-makers, while owners of private coaches might send out a footman ahead with an axe to clear a way through. An Act of 1663 permitted turnpikes to be established

Husband and wife travelling

to pay for road repair, but little use was made of it, though Celia Fiennes, the intrepid lady traveller who wrote about her journeys at the end of the seventeenth century, recorded that passengers along a causeway in Norfolk paid 'a penny a horse in order to the mending the way, for all about is not to be rode on unless it's a very dry summer'; nevertheless the causeway was full of holes. So travel by road was an adventure rather than a pleasure. 'Riders fell from their horses with alarming frequency; coaches were overturned, were left stranded amid quicksand, and lost in floodwaters' (Joan Parkes). Highwaymen and robbers were numerous, even as near to London as Hampstead Heath or Shooters Hill in Kent.

It was said that the best roads in England were in Norfolk and the worst in the west of England, though, surprisingly, many of the roads in Sussex and Kent were poor. As it was always raining in the west of England travel there, as also in the extreme north, was usually adventurous and slow. Celia Fiennes, who did not do much grumbling, complained of the way from Launceston to Exeter, 'its narrow lanes full of stones and loose ground clay'; the 'stony and dirty' lanes around Axminster she also found annoying, while in Cornwall she discovered the people were 'very ill guides, and know but little from home, only to some market town they frequent, but will be very solicitous to know where you go, and how far, and from whence you came, and where is your abode'.

The safest way to travel was on horse or foot. Horses could be hired at inns and by regularly changing mounts the traveller in a hurry might achieve a fair speed. Horses were kept by postmasters on the principal highways out of London to facilitate the delivery of the royal mails and travellers could usually get hold of post horses, though at the outset of the period no one was supposed to 'ride post' except in the company of a guide blowing his horn. This no doubt was a method only for V.I.P.s. But postmasters found the hiring out of horses a profitable side-line and the privilege of being a postmaster was valued by innkeepers.

Travellers outside an inn

In the reign of Charles I the inland and foreign posts had been combined under the control of one postmaster, Thomas Witherings, who was the father of the Post Office in its modern form. Under his reorganization scheme regular posts, available to everyone, set out along the main roads from London, the postboys dropping their bags at the larger towns as they went; from these towns bags would be carried to neighbouring villages, each having its own post-master who would then send out postboys blowing their horns and delivering their letters. A General Letter Office was then set up in Lombard Street. Postal fees varied; Witherings charged 2d. to send a letter 80 miles; in 1680 the first penny post was set up in the London area by an enterprising independent undertaker, William Docwra, but was later taken over and embodied into the general postal system. It was not, however, until the reign of William and Mary that 'cross posts' were arranged between

A postboy

A coach

important towns without touching London. Earlier in the Stuart period all letters had to go through London: thus the Government found it fairly easy to keep a check on treasonable conspirators who unwisely used the public postal services.

This gradual expansion of the postal service meant that horses became more readily available for hire, since the numerous local postmasters were allowed to let out their horses when they were not required for the postmen. The traveller might be charged 3*d.* or 4*d.* a mile for the hire of a horse and would have to pay an additional sixpence for a postilion or guide. But the postmasters never had an effective monopoly in hiring out horses; and in fact the cost of travel by horse was determined by supply and demand.

Coaches had been used in the reign of Elizabeth I, but the first stage coaches were introduced early in the Stuart age. A hackney-coach rank was formed in the Strand in 1634 and stage coaches began business about the middle of the seventeenth century. Journeys by stage or private coach were usually extremely slow, as was understandable enough in view of the state of the roads. Even in the reign of William III when James Brydges was obliged to take the stage coach from Stanmore to the City of London because his own coach had broken down, it took him four to six hours to do the trip. A 'flying coach' which operated between London and Oxford, the proprietors boasted, could do the journey in a day; the Cirencester flying coach also did the 91 miles to London in a day during the reign of Queen Anne; but in general such journeys by coach took longer.

Noblemen and weathy gentlemen would have their own coaches as a matter of social prestige and would show them off by driving around Hyde Park in them. Such coaches would have six, eight, or even 12 horses; sometimes elaborate and beautiful vehicles were imported from abroad for royal or noble use. In the reign of Charles II Samuel Pepys owned his own coach and was delighted when 'the people did mightily look upon it'. But travel by coach was cumbersome and clumsy and often extremely uncomfortable, for these coaches rarely had springs. In London the hackney coaches were described as 'hackney hell carts' and those who sat on the 'boot' in a stage coach were pretty well resigned to road sickness.

A popular method of travel was by water; though there were as yet no canals, many navigable rivers existed; travel by barge or rowing boat on the Thames was as a rule quicker than by coach or even by horse. Wherrymen are known also to have provided services on the Severn. But this method of travel was dependent on the availability of watermen, while serious risks attached to the weather. In February 1692, 11 out of 17 passengers in a boat going down the river Thames during one of the several severe frosts of the century were found dead in the boat next morning, according to Nicholas Luttrell, because of 'the severity of the weather'.

Nevertheless the difficulties and dangers of moving about Stuart England need not be exaggerated. Celia Fiennes, who travelled about 3,000 miles around England, had not many complaints to record; George Fox, who rode widely upon his missionary work as a leading Quaker, mentions few natural obstacles. Well-to-do gentlemen like John Evelyn, who were

The Thames during the Great Frost of 1677

Pack-horses

provided with plenty of horses and servants, thought nothing of travelling around the kingdom or moving regularly between their country houses and the capital. A country surgeon like James Yonge went up and down to London without any serious mishaps. In the summer of 1619 a traveller succeeded for a bet in getting from London to Calais and back between dawn and dusk. The Dover and Harwich roads had good reputations. Others besides Celia Fiennes, from John Taylor, the 'water poet', to Daniel Defoe, the reporter, travelled widely about the country, while foreign visitors rarely omitted visits to Canterbury, Oxford and Cambridge, as well as to the capital. The carriage of letters and parcels by packhorse was increasingly better organized, though naturally the service was more regular in the larger towns. All transport was obviously liable to be interrupted by bad weather; but then the same is true in our own more advanced age.

TRAVELLING ABROAD

Englishmen travelled abroad both on business and on pleasure in order to broaden their minds or complete their education. While a licence was required to go overseas, there was rarely much difficulty in evading the authorities. During the Interregnum Royalists got in and out of the country ruled by the Cromwells with a fair degree of ease: the Earl of Ormonde went backwards and forwards to London from Flanders in disguise. At other times daring Roman Catholic priests entered and left the country on their various missions, though their lives were forfeit if they were caught. It was almost impossible for a guard to be kept over all the beaches and coves near which a vessel might anchor. But there were regular services of packetboats and these were always greeted and watched by hordes of

162

officials and others on the make when they docked on either
side. The regular route to France was from Dover to Calais,
to Holland from Harwich, and to Spain from Falmouth. The
fare across the Channel was 5s. and the trip was supposed to
take three hours. In fact the charges mounted up in one way or
another, and it cost an additional 5s. or more for a cabin in the
stern. The boats, which were only of 60 tons, were crowded
and slow. On one occasion William Congreve persuaded some
Frenchmen to row him across the Channel and he did the journey
from Dover to Calais more quickly than if he had waited for
the packet-boat.

Although traders must have travelled extensively, our knowledge of Englishmen abroad largely concerns ambassadors, the
aristocracy and their attendants. In the reign of James I
embassies existed at Paris and The Hague, while there were
usually residents at Venice and Turin, Madrid and Brussels,
and often in Constantinople and Rome. To be an ambassador
was quite a professional undertaking, even if or perhaps because
he was regarded as a 'great spy' or merchant adventurer. To
be on an ambassador's staff was to be on the road to preferment.
For example, one Bullen Reymes, who played his lute persuasively for the benefit of two English diplomatic representatives
in Italy, ultimately secured personal advancement. During the

The cross-channel port of Harwich

Foreign travel

years when England was not at war with France the English ambassador in Paris was an important figure; so on occasions were the ambassadors in Holland. But the slowness of the posts made it hard for English representatives farther afield to do much more than watch over and entertain the important personages who passed their way.

It seems that more Englishmen travelled abroad during the Stuart period than the Elizabethan. The Earl of Clarendon noted in his retirement abroad after 1667 that a change had come over Europe; for in his father's time travel was unusual except for merchants and 'gentlemen who resolved to be soldiers'. The commonest travellers seem to have been young noblemen who, in order to prepare themselves for their responsibilities at Court, either made the Grand Tour of France or the Giro d'Italia. Considerable risks attached to travel and it was also expensive. It was reckoned to cost £1,000 a year to travel around Italy and it was always possible that a rich young man might be waylaid and murdered. Though some Englishmen might have conscientiously described in their diaries the beauties and customs of foreign lands or have carried on their studies in foreign cities, others were mainly absorbed in enjoying themselves as the chances offered. A contrast can be seen between the jottings of John Evelyn who travelled widely during the civil wars and those of John Reresby who was abroad at about the same time and got up to all sorts of mischief with his friend. Evelyn spent much of his time in Paris listening to English sermons; Reresby worked on mathematics as well as fencing and dancing while he was in Venice, but his

164

companion, John Berry dallied with an Italian mistress. Sir William Trumbull, who was later to become an English ambassador in Paris observed: 'I went abroad and spent about two years in France and Italy where I learnt little besides the languages, partly from my youth and the warmth of my temper, partly from laziness and debauchery.'

Most young noblemen were accompanied by clerical tutors, who might in the long run benefit from their knowledge and experience, even though they were little more than servants. Inigo Jones, as has been noted, accompanied the Earl of Arundel to Italy and later Thomas Hobbes, the philosopher, was a tutor to Sir William Cavendish, afterwards second Earl of Devonshire, in France and Italy. Such tutors were rarely successful in keeping their masters out of scrapes. English ambassadors in France complained of the amount of duelling that went on. In 1609 Sir George Carew wrote from Paris: 'I am still much troubled here about the quarrels of the young gentlemen of our nation.' In the course of such quarrels in France and Italy several young Englishmen got themselves killed. On the whole, these travellers were men of much the same characters and habits, and followed the same established routes: Paris and Lyons, Venice and Padua were favourite stopping-places, but it was considered rather daring to go to Rome or Madrid. Roman Catholic priests were said to be always on the look-out for conversions of the influential English travellers; a determined effort was made to induce Charles I to change his religion when he was in Madrid before he became king.

Some students of the time took the view that the effects of foreign travel were always bad; others insisted that it did in fact widen men's outlooks. Much depended on the calibre of the individual. It is not unfair to contrast with the young noblemen for whom the Grand Tour was a jaunt a hard-working young gentleman like John Verney, the younger son of Sir Ralph Verney of Buckinghamshire. John's father wanted him to go to the Bar, but after leaving his private school in Kensington the youth himself begged to become a merchant. His father was persuaded to apprentice him for the sum of £400 for seven years to Gabriel Roberts, a silk merchant in the Levant Company, since he realized that it was 'no disparagement for the younger son of a squire to become a merchant of foreign commerce'. After working for nearly two years in Mr Roberts's back shop in the City, where the bales of silk were weighed, John Verney was dispatched in a Smyrna ship, part of a convoy sailing to Aleppo in Syria, then part of the Turkish empire. Here amid the flat white roofs and mosques Verney completed his term of apprenticeship and at the end of it he was made a partner in the firm, which at its English factory in Aleppo, exchanged English cloths, lead and tin, and re-exports from the Far East for the silks and other rarities of Asia. Verney stayed on there for another five years, the monotony of his exile relieved only by visits to the Holy Land and to Cyprus and by playing the guitar or taking rides before sunset. Before his return home 150,000 were killed by a visitation of the plague to the Middle East and he and his fellow factors experienced locusts in the summer and snows in the winter. So he passed a total of 15 years of his life away from his home. He returned to England at the age of 32 to marry and settle down, to become really wealthy and a leading figure in the City of London. He was indeed a true merchant adventurer.

Yet though it was men like John Verney who built up the nation's wealth and enriched the life of the English people of his time, certainly the cosmopolitan character of the arts in England under the Stuarts owed a good deal to the more numerous and leisurely noble travellers as well as to the exile of the Court in the middle of the seventeenth century. At the close of the Stuart age the presence of English armies in the Netherlands helped Dutch inventions and ideas to penetrate into England.

MOTIVES FOR COLONIZATION

Just as mixed motives induced Englishmen to visit the mainland of Europe, so many different explanations are offered for the urge in the Stuart age to seek little known or unexplored places. Some men were genuinely adventurous, expecting to make their fortunes. They had read about the voyages of Drake and Raleigh in the Elizabethan age and hoped to find an Eldorado full of gold and silver mines that would enable them to live as idly as a Spanish Grandee. In fact most of the really profitable business was done by hard work through the trading companies, like the Levant, the East India and the Royal Africa Companies and several others. A number of merchants and their friends grew rich through judicious investments in these companies, some of which were run on a joint-stock principle for each voyage undertaken: a share in a ship that carried

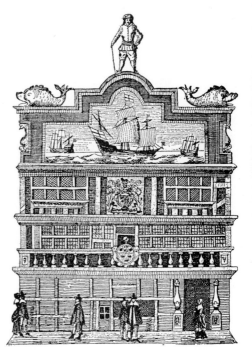

East India House, in Leadenhall Street, built 1648

back a saleable cargo might be very rewarding indeed. Spices from India, currants from Greece, timber from the Baltic lands, silks from Asia, ivory and slaves from Africa—all met a sure demand. The older companies like the Merchant Adventurers would have permanent agents at Bremen, Antwerp or Amsterdam to do their business, but daring men would range farther to Russia, say, or Crete. The period of comparative peace that followed the accession of James I to the English throne and the accumulation of capital by landowners and sheepmasters opened the opportunity for investments in permanent plantations in unpopulated parts of the globe that might lead the way to valuable returns both for the colonists themselves and for those ready to sponsor them.

What were the other motives of the Englishmen who ventured overseas in the Stuart age? Apart from the gambling spirit that induced them to seek for quick untapped new sources of wealth, there was the insatiable desire for land that was deliberately fostered by the promoters of colonization. An American prospectus of 1622 said:

> With what content shall the particular person employ himself there when he shall find that for £12 10s. adventure he shall be made lord of 200 acres, to him and his heirs forever. And for the charge of transportation of himself, his family and tenants he shall be allotted for every person he carries 100 acres more. And what labourer soever transport himself thither at his own charge to have the like proportion of land upon the aforesaid conditions and be sure of employment to his good content for present maintenance.

Undoubtedly the hope of finding vast cultivable lands in the New World tempted many colonists, who were discontented with their lot at home. Poor men even undertook years of servitude to pay for their passage in the hope of winning free land. Imaginations were stirred by such prospectuses, books, and tales of the luxuriant plenty that awaited the colonial adventurer. These pioneers might not have overlooked the terrors of the actual journey across the Atlantic. But when they at last reached the promised land, whether it was Virginia (first colonized in 1607), New Plymouth, or Massachusetts, they were in for many disappointments. Only sheer grilling hard work enabled the colonists to overcome the natural obstacles and the diseases, the mosquitoes, and the rattlesnakes, to cut their way through the huge forests, and to resist the Indians. When the truth got out in the first half of the seventeenth century, it was less easy to persuade more colonists to go. Only an occasional shipload of supplies or of marriageable women preserved New England from complete collapse in its pioneering days. And volunteers were supplemented by the transportation of criminals and vagrants and even unwanted children, notably to Virginia and the West Indies.

Who were the other migrants? It has been estimated that some 20,000 Englishmen and women crossed the Atlantic up to the outbreak of the civil wars. Were the motives of the settlers more religious than economic as it has sometimes been suggested? It is perfectly true that a number of families that went were of a dissenting frame of mind and disliked the High

Quakers emigrating

Church government of Archbishop Laud. But they did not go out there primarily to set up nonconformist commonwealths in the New World or with the aim of a major conversion of the 'Red Indians'. What happened was that many of the merchants who interested themselves in establishing colonies and provided the funds for doing so were themselves Puritans and therefore ready to pay for suitable ministers to accompany the colonists to their new homes. Typical of such merchants was Matthew Cradock, the Governor of the Massachusetts Bay Company. One of the Ministers sent out by his company was Thomas Higginson. According to Cotton Mather, when the boat on which Higginson sailed was passing Land's End he called together his fellow passengers to take their last sight of England and said:

> We will not say as the separatists were wont to say at their leaving of England, Farewell, Babylon! Farewell, Rome! But we will say, farewell, dear England! Farewell the Church of God in England, and all the Christian friends there! We do not go to New England as separatists from the Church of England; though we cannot but separate from the corruptions in it. But we go to practise the positive part of the church reformation, and propagate the gospel in America.

The arguments put forward by John Winthrop, a Puritan lawyer who was to become Governor of Massachusetts, were that colonization was a service to the Protestant Church because it raised a bulwark against the Jesuits, that England was overcrowded, that the poor were a great burden to it, and that good land was available for everyone in the New World. In fact the majority of the first emigrants were comparatively poor people —only a handful of yeomen were to be found among them— who left home for overseas because they hoped for better things.

William Penn (1644-1718)

Winthrop's own sister felt doubts about the wisdom of going to America lest it should lower their social status. And in fact some of the upper classes who went, like Sir Henry Vane, and some of the ministers, like Hugh Peter, who afterwards became one of Cromwell's chaplains, did not stay very long. Massachusetts proved rather narrow in its outlook—indeed it was out of its exiles that the colony of Rhode Island was largely built; Maryland was colonized under the direction of its proprietor, Lord Baltimore, a Roman Catholic, who allowed religious freedom to all, and it was the Bermudas rather than the settlements on the American mainland which in the early Stuart age was the greatest Puritan colony. Later in the century William Penn the Quaker, who accepted a grant of land from Charles II in return for a debt owed to his father, opened a colony for nonconformists, where for a time the Puritan spirit as well as Puritan business enterprise flourished.

But the chief aim of nearly all these colonists was economic improvement; and at first it was the Bermudas and Barbados rather than Virginia and New England where the prospects appeared brightest. Sir George Somers, who accidentally discovered Bermuda, thought it 'the most beautiful place he ever came to, for fish, hogs, and fowl', while a sea captain, Richard Moore, who went there with a load of settlers, noted the numbers of sperm whales, palm and cedar trees, and tobacco plants, and declared these were indeed peaceful and enchanted islands. Barbados did an active trade with New England and the island was to become the home of rich planters rejoicing in the sugar crops and at a time in buccaneering expeditions against the Spaniards. As the colonial prospects became more promising the character of the emigrants began to change. It has been stated that after 1642 the Puritan exodus from England slackened and Cavalier and middle-class immigrants transformed the complexion of Virginia. The most famous of Virginians, George Washington, the father of his country, was the descendant of a small Northamptonshire squire.

By the end of the Stuart period 12 out of the 13 original American colonies had been established; the West Indies, including Jamaica, conquered by Cromwell, and the Bermudas were flourishing; a busy trade was being done with India and Africa; and Hudson's Bay, Nova Scotia, and Newfoundland had become British. Thus, after much turmoil and suffering, many tragedies and sudden deaths, those Englishmen who had been prepared to sail across the seas in search of new lands to live in or new trades to follow or merely the right to practise their own form of Christianity in peace, had obtained their rewards, if not for themselves, then at least for their children and children's children.

Life in England under the Stuarts, as was pointed out at the beginning of this book, was hard for the mass of the people. Though a richer and more peaceful prospect was to dawn after the long wars with France that ended in 1713, the deep contrast

The English in Virginia

between the lives of rich and poor remained unaltered. Wealth was increasingly concentrated in the hands of comparatively few—the nobility and big landed gentry, the successful merchants, and the rising professional classes, while the town and village labourers looked back on a century or more which had witnessed many wars, spells of unemployment, much sickness, malnutrition, and endemic poverty. It was no wonder that the more venturesome among the ordinary people of England embraced such opportunities as they were offered to emigrate to a new world, which beckoned them no longer with a mirage of gold, but with a vision of virgin fields that they might cultivate in a spirit of freedom and equality for the benefit of themselves, their families and their posterity. Englishmen might, on the whole, have been lazy and content to let things drift on much as they had done before; but among them there were always plenty of gamblers. And for some at least of those who staked their lives and savings in the Stuart age, the gamble paid off.

Further Reading

C. M. Andrews, *The Colonial Period of American History*, 1, 1934
Allen French, *Charles I and the Puritan Upheaval*, 1955
Christopher Morris (ed.), *The Journeys of Celia Fiennes*, 1947
Joan Parkes, *Travel in England in the Seventeenth Century* (illustrated), 1925
J. W. Stoye, *English Travelling Abroad, 1604–1667*, 1952
Margaret M. Verney (ed.), *Memoirs of the Verney Family*, Vols. III and IV, 1894 and 1899
J. A. Williamson, *A Short History of British Expansion*, 1953

Index

The numerals in **heavy type** refer to the page numbers of the illustrations